BEFORE THE HAMMER FALLS

THE INSIDER'S GUIDE TO
PROPERTY AUCTION SUCCESS

JAY HOWARD & PIOTR RUSINEK

First published in 2019 by
Howard Rusinek Consulting Ltd

PB 978-1-912892-36-5
eBook 978-1-912892-37-2

Project management by whitefox
Designed and typeset by seagulls.net

Printed and bound in Szczecin, Poland by ZAPOL Sobczyk Sp.J.

CONTENTS

DISCLAIMER – OUR NOD TO THE LEGAL EAGLES AND THE FINANCIAL FALCONS

This book seeks to provide you with the necessary tools and information required to approach the auction with an increased degree of confidence and responsibility in your buying and selling activity.

We have provided the basic elements of the auction for your consideration and we have, where possible, expanded on those principles based on our collected skill, knowledge and extensive experience.

With that in mind, the disclaimer is in place to highlight how tempestuous property, the auction market, an individual's experience, property strategy and the advent of new concepts can be and can cause to undermine or make outdated the various principles explained within this book.

Our intention is to offer general guidance, to help progress your auction property journey, your property journey in general and your property success. The contents of this book provide no substitute for professional legal or financial (regulated or unregulated) advice.

No responsibility for loss or damage on, for, or on behalf of any party as a result of the content published in this book can be attributed to the authors. Therefore, any use of this content is at the reader's own risk and at their own discretion.

Neither the publishers nor the authors will accept any liability for any damages, loss or claim for any use or misuse of the information provided in this book.

Furthermore, no responsibility will be accepted by the authors or the publishers for any views or content provided by any third-party contributors.

FOREWORD

by Martin Skinner – CEO of Inspired Asset Management

Auctions have always been close to my heart. When I sourced through auctions, I would look through around 1,400 listings every month giving the most interesting ones a hot/warm/ cold rating. I typically looked for potential to add value through extra bedrooms, extra units, and the ability to do this quickly through permitted development rights. The ability to add value is a must when purchasing through auction and key to any successful strategy. This is how I built Inspired and Nice Group previously.

When buying at auction you need to be aware of a lot of pitfalls. Auctions are known to be a dumping ground for problem properties. I vividly remember a particular problem property. It was a piece of land adjoining an end-terrace property. The land had planning for an additional dwelling. However, the special conditions contained a clause referring to another condition. Only after a careful check by my solicitor, minutes before the bidding was about to commence, we realised this related to a restrictive covenant stating the land was only to be used as a single dwelling. We realised that included the existing house next door and we would never be able to develop that land. Someone else bought it for £400,000 and it turned out to be a very expensive garden! It still sits empty.

The safest properties are usually stock-sold by public sector entities such as housing associations, councils, plc companies and government entities because they are normally clear of major issues. There are more problems with properties offered by private sellers.

I have developed over £500m worth of property comprising over 3,500 units for rent and sale – most of which was delivered through office-residential permitted development conversions. However, office-to-resi has become extremely competitive and it's hard to find properties where, after all risks are accounted for, we can achieve a satisfactory margin on cost. It's a sign that the market is turning, and an experienced investor would always turn to where there is exit liquidity and appropriate risk-adjusted return. For that reason, I'm now going back to auctions to look for deals where I can add value and exit quickly with a good profit.

Auctions give the ability to follow the market extremely closely as transactions are happening right there in the auction room. The best advice I'd give to people considering auctions: work hard and persevere because it's a numbers (practice) game, get creative and make lots of friends. You're going to need them when things go wrong, and you'll want to celebrate with them when things go well!

I think a book like this will help people to approach auctions with an equal degree of confidence and caution – it really is a must-read for those looking to be successful in the property world.

CHAPTER 1
INTRODUCTION

Personal note from the Authors....

We appreciate your interest in our book.

We wish you success in your Personal

and Professional LIFE.

ABOUT THE AUTHORS

@the.auction.insider Jay Howard has been active within the property industry for the past fifteen years, starting his professional career with a high street estate agent, then moving into the world of property development, trust fund and asset management and most recently extending his knowledge and experience within the auction industry. Jay has the benefit of three degrees (Psychology, Classics and Law), the knowledge of which adds value to his experience and understanding on an ongoing basis.

@the.auction.pro Piotr Rusinek has been a London-based property investor specialising in the property auctions market for the past seven years, establishing himself as a knowledgeable and trustworthy partner to his clients. Over this period, Piotr has bought and sold properties worth more than fifteen million pounds for his investors and himself, and in 2016 was one of the top performers on Simon Zutshi's Property Mastermind Programme. He has presented on the topic of auctions to thousands of investors, continuing to do so on a monthly basis, and has invested large amounts of time and effort in achieving this recognisable position within the industry. His keen property sense and his ability to locate investment properties is boundless in its value.

WHY WE WROTE THIS BOOK

@the.auction.pro I have been working with clients for many years and a lot of my conversations are around the same auction subjects and principles. My primary intention for this book is to put them together as reference points that anyone can draw from and to mitigate risks when it comes to auction transactions.

I made my name by helping clients and joint venture partners buy and sell properties through auctions. One of the most important things in all of those transactions is the trust that both parties have in each other and in the process. This is probably relevant to any industry where the velocity with which things are happening is high. Without trust in the process and people that are on your team, you will not go far. You also need to know which things to question, and when, in order to make the deals happen without taking unnecessary risks. I hope this book will provide you with the information on how to tackle each auction step and make you a successful investor or trader.

@the.auction.insider In June of 2018, I was approached by my co-author with the idea of writing a book on property auctions. I had not thought of writing a book like this before. With the blessings and support of my directors, Jamie Royston and Andrew Binstock at Auction House London, we started to write this book in August of 2018, and completed the final draft in January 2019.

My primary motivation in writing this book has been to educate. Sadly, in my work, you see people buying properties when they haven't conducted any due diligence whatsoever. I think that auctions are a great vehicle to purchase property and I would like to make it far more approachable for a wider audience. A lot of what we have written is based on practical application and specific knowledge-based sense.

I believe that this book will arm you with sufficient knowledge to find, research, bid on and buy a property at auction. I hope this book will be of some use to seasoned and starter property professionals, as well as the owner/occupier just looking to make their way onto the property ladder. I have gone into some specific detail within the book whilst trying to make the book approachable to new property investors and owner/purchasers. For me, this is very much a one-stop 'how to' guide on property auctions.

I am passionate about property auctions and property in general. I feel that there is a real dearth of knowledge and information out there which is readily accessible, and which is presented from two very unique perspectives. I think what I know is learnable and useable, which is why we wrote this book. The auction is such a brilliant way for the buyers to interact with the property market and fantastic opportunities at a discount to the open market.

There are many things that I would like to see change within the auction industry. All of these changes I think will make us far more approachable and a far more viable option to the market at large. I think we need to consider the confusion and disparity between the guide price and the reserve price. I like the idea of disclosing a starting bid; this will help people know where they stand on the day of the auction and can give them a reasonable expectation of sales price. In general, I think that the property industry needs the same kind of overhaul that the legal services industry went through about ten years ago. I think this will improve public perception and confidence in the process.

@the.auction.pro As above! I am known for taking some risks, but also known for walking away from deals that would have made hundreds of thousands of pounds in profits – only because some vital information was missing, and I did not want to take an unknown risk that could potentially cause significant losses! Hence, take this book as an informational guide and trust your professional team of solicitors, accountants, brokers and others who have the necessary knowledge and indemnity insurance to advise you safely on particular transactions. Having a team who can perform under auction timelines is extremely valuable. If you have a team like that already, make sure you pay them well and stick with them. If, however, you are looking for a team, feel free to use the partners who helped me in my investing journey and who are featured in this book.

@the.auction.insider We have selected a handful of recommended service providers whose details are shared at the end of this chapter, within the book and on the rear cover. All you need to do is quote 'Before the Hammer Falls' and someone will be able to offer you a professional and friendly service. If you have any specific enquiries or questions about anything covered in this book, please reach out to me and Piotr through our contact details below, or on social media.

HOW TO READ THIS BOOK

This book is intended to be a 'How to' guide to property auctions, with added commentary from both Jay and Piotr. The content of each chapter will be an interchangeable narration from either Jay **@the.auction.insider** or Piotr **@the.auction.pro**.

Chapters 1 to 4 follow the auction process, allowing you to get comfortable with the property scene and opening you up to networks of people who can be helpful on your property journey.

Chapters 5 to 13 deal with the phases of the auction process from the purchasing perspective. They will contain an explanation, case studies and useful tips for dealing with certain circumstances.

Chapter 14 is an introduction to modern methods of selling, i.e. online auctions.

Chapter 15 is for those who would like to consider selling their property at auction.

Then there are three bonus chapters going deeper into specific subjects: underwriting, due diligence and multiple exits.

We hope you will find reading this book educational, worthwhile and rewarding.

Legal services partner's content (page 136):
Ronald Fletcher Baker LLP
www.rfblegal.co.uk 020 7467 5757

Financial services partner's content (page 171):
Mortgage Desk
www.mortgage-desk.com 01296 329 620

Insurance Services partner's content (page 151):
Insurance Desk
http://www.insurance-desk.com 01296 329 610

Piotr's social media:
www.facebook.com/the.auction.pro
www.instagram.com/the.auction.pro/
www.linkedin.com/in/theauctionpro/

Jay's social media:
www.facebook.com/the.auction.insider
www.instagram.com/the.auction.insider
www.linkedin.com/in/theauctioninsider

CHAPTER 2
WHAT'S ALL THE FUSS ABOUT – WHY BUY AT AUCTION?

@the.auction.insider I'll start by saying that I am evangelical about auctions. It can be argued successfully that I take this view because I work within the industry and am passionate about what I do. What isn't very well known is my interactions with property auctions before I started working in the auction market and, equally so, my continued approach to auctions and utilising my investment strategy, which relies heavily on access to the auction market.

@the.auction.pro My background is in sourcing properties for investors and developers in London. That is how I started my career. The biggest frustration of my work was that it would sometimes take six to eighteen months for certain transactions to go through the legal process and it wasn't unusual that some of them would fall through just before exchanging the contracts. This is in contrast to auctions where the deal is done (or not done) within two or three weeks. This is an enormous advantage of auctions from the purchaser's perspective, especially in a rising market like the one we experienced in 2011–2015. Anyone could get gazumped, as prices kept rising every month. Auctions give certainty in any market – they tend to be fair for both buyers and sellers. And auctions are a perfect place to find problem properties – i.e. the kind of properties that have defects that scare away most of the buyers and where agents don't know how to handle them. These types of properties eventually end up in auctions at a low price and, if you know what the problems are and how to solve them, they provide a great opportunity to increase value with some paper exercise or skilful negotiations. @the.auction.insider has given most of the reasons why buying in auctions is a great idea.

UNFETTERED ACCESS TO OPPORTUNITY

@the.auction.insider This is one of the things that I love about auctions; that they are open and available to all, without restriction or conditions. If you are in the market to buy a property, you will be given an equal and fair opportunity to access the market.

One of the reasons I love working where I do is because this principle is held in very high regard. All registered parties are kept up-to-date at all points along the property's journey (notification of viewings, additional viewings, the legal pack, pre-auction offers etc. ...). This means that all parties have the same access to information and can make a fair and reasonable decision based on that information.

We make public as much information as is possible to ensure that all parties have the same level of access and information, and because it is public (catalogue, website, legal pack and addendum), all are given equal opportunity.

PRICE INCENTIVE

This is possibly the biggest reason why people look for a purchase at auction. Whilst it is certainly a major consideration to purchasers, do not be fooled on price – there are other considerations. Whilst we are talking price, below are a couple of things to take into consideration when looking at a property which is guided and reserved well below the perceived market value:

1 **The property requires a programme of refurbishment/ modernisation/structural work etc.** This is possibly the most considered approach to accessing a bargain at the auction. Find a property that requires one of the above, conduct the necessary works and re-sell (or rent out) for a profit. It is worth mentioning here that profit isn't the only consideration; you are creating a home and access to the property market for a person a rung or two below you on the property ladder – this should be considered a service and delivered exceptionally for true value, both to you and your eventual purchaser.

2 **The property with the development angle/change of use/ extension/sub-division etc.** This is considered more appropriate for the professional purchaser, as it will in some respect or another encompass the point above. But this option is far trickier to navigate successfully, insofar as the knowledge and experience required to implement the above opportunities can be more complex. They normally require

the knowledge and experience to cost a development, the ability to navigate local planning guidelines and the legal knowledge required to sub-divide a property whilst increasing value and access to your end user market.

3 **The property with the legal issue, be it adverse possession/ an enforcement notice/boundary disputes etc.** I like these opportunities, because they normally require an element of problem solving, but more so, there are processes in place which can mitigate the scare factors. For instance, the adverse possession option – you need to ask yourself several questions before you proceed; for instance, was there a tenancy agreement in place at some stage? Is there rent being paid? How long has the adverse occupant been in occupation? These questions will mitigate your risk and point you in the right direction to solve the problem, therefore allowing you to re-sell or re-rent the property at a full value. Likewise with the enforcement notice. When was the enforcement notice issued? Is there a fine attached to the notice? Can the notice be remedied? Can the notice be appealed? All are useful questions to help you decide whether you choose to proceed and at what level.

4 **The property with the procedural issue, whereby the property has a short leasehold interest/forfeiture notice/ elapsed planning.** I'm not sure how many people would have dealt with a short leasehold purchase. The process is quite simple, but requires negotiation and persistence. The matter can become trickier if the leasehold interest has less than seventy years remaining, and even more so if there is

an absentee freeholder. There are, of course, multiple ways to overcome these issues, but most will require time and the employment of professionals to resolve. Add these costs in when considering your maximum bid price. The same can be said for a forfeiture notice, but without a shadow of a doubt, you will require a practised solicitor in such matters – they will be worth their weight in gold.

You can see from the above that there are multiple reasons why a property may be guided and reserved low. Remember that the property has been discounted from the perceived market value to start with and then discounted further to take any number of these (and many other) potential issues into consideration. In truth, that is why the auction is a market for added value buyers, problem solvers, investors, developers and more recently owner/occupiers – the potential and access for opportunity is immense; it brings (generally speaking) unmarketable, unsaleable and unmortgageable properties into the market place and provides the opportunity for those properties to be revitalised and more importantly, to be made accessible to the wider property market for the consideration of a far wider group of potential buyers.

UNMORTGAGEABLE PROPERTIES

Below is a short list of examples which can generally affect the mortgageability of a property:

- A property with no kitchen or bathroom.
- A derelict property (depending on the length of time it has been derelict).
- A property with prominent or dangerous structural issues.
- Short leasehold flats (generally with seventy years or less remaining on the lease).
- A property with a purchase price or valuation less than £50,000 (in some cases even as low as £40,000; this can affect buy-to-let mortgages especially).
- A property with a defect within the lease (this could be a forfeiture, a doubling ground rent at an unreasonable rate and charge or an absentee freeholder).
- A property with adverse possession (life tenancies at nil rent, regulated tenancies, assured tenancies, protected tenancies, sitting tenants or squatters).
- A property of non-standard construction (concrete construction, timber frame construction and properties with asbestos).

There can be far more reasons, but different lenders will have different requirements and products. The above is just a good start and a good indication as to what might affect a property's mortgageability.

SPEED IS THE KEY

An auction can come and go in the blink of an eye. Most auction companies will run anywhere between five to ten auctions a year. Generally speaking, in January and August there will be no auctions, but there are one or two exceptions to the rule. An auction company that runs an auction generally seven times a year will be working around a seven-week cycle (assuming they are not running an auction in January or August). This means that there are roughly three and a half weeks to add properties to the auction (to create the catalogue) and three and a half weeks to market the properties (viewings and legal packs), which lead up to a single day of sales.

Upon the exchange of contracts on the day of the auction, you will have twenty-eight days (or twenty working days) to complete on your purchase. There are one or two exceptions to the rule and these exceptions offer a great deal of insight and opportunity — for example, most repossession sales can have a completion timeline of ten to fourteen days to complete. Similarly, if the property is being sold by a receiver, the completion in some cases can be six to twelve weeks.

Do not be dissuaded from the auction because the timescale is short, especially where there is an advantage to be gained. Putting yourself in a position to purchase a property within a shorter timeline makes you think and investigate the property in greater depth in advance of the auction — this is something that is transferable to the rest of your property journey and can encourage you to build a defined due diligence process. In addition to this, although the low price of the property is likely to be attractive to many potential buyers, the short timescale might reduce your competition. This is definitely something to take advantage of.

The speed of the transaction comes with a degree of certainty (discussed below). If you are running your property investments as a business, this requirement of speed is a great tool for you. It means that you can exchange on a property, complete on the property and have works started within four weeks. If you have an active pipeline or are thinking of starting an active pipeline, then the auction is a great way to keep your pipeline busy and reduces the number of fall-throughs.

INCREASED CERTAINTY OF SALE

For all who have experienced the following, you truly have my sympathies. You also have my blessing to switch over to the auction model to alleviate or dramatically reduce these issues from plaguing your property journey. At some stage or another, you are likely to experience one of the following:

1   **Gazumping:** This is a fairly standard scenario; you see a property on the market, you conduct your research and you make an offer. The seller accepts your offer and you instruct a solicitor and a surveyor. You agree the terms upon which the transaction can take place and proceed to exchange contracts. All of a sudden, things go quiet and you ask your solicitor to chase the other side's solicitor. You find out that another party has made a higher offer, which has now been accepted (this scenario happens both pre- and post-exchange of contracts). In this situation, you are now induced to either re-negotiate or walk away from

the purchase, potentially writing off your time and effort to date, as well as your abortive costs in relation to your solicitor and the surveyor's fees.

2   **Gazundering:** In this scenario, your roles are reversed. You are now the seller, and a potential purchaser has made an offer, which you have accepted. The agent removes the property from the market and you progress to exchange and completion. The buyer instructs their solicitors and a surveyor – and something in the survey causes the buyer to reduce their offer (indeed, they can reduce their offer for any number of reasons, but this is a good scenario and happens to be one of the largest culprits of gazundering). In this situation, you have a few options: you can accept the reduced price for the reasons provided, you can negotiate an amount between the original price and the newly submitted price, or you can pull out of the sale and re-market.

I know that in recent years, savvy solicitors have been adding abortive costs to the heads of terms, including a clause for abortive costs should either one of the above scenarios occur. The auction, however, fixes the price at the moment the auctioneer declares that the property has sold and bangs the gavel. This is the legal exchange of contracts with a 10 per cent non-refundable deposit (this can vary; on low value lots – normally on transactions below £40,000 – there can be a fixed deposit price of £5,000 or £8,000). This ensures that the buyer and seller are significantly invested in the purchase of the property.

If the sale fails to complete, there are several things that can happen. If, for instance, the seller fails to complete, the buyer can put the seller on notice to complete. If they fail to complete after that, then the buyer can have their full deposit returned, along with the buyer's fee from the seller. Alternatively, they can sue for specific performance of the contract, in an attempt to enforce the contract and proceed to completion. Likewise, if it is the buyer who fails to complete, the seller can serve them with a notice to complete. If they fail to complete, the deposit becomes forfeit and the buyer loses their deposit. Additionally, the seller can re-sell the property, and if it sells for a lesser price the second time around, the seller can pursue the original buyer for the difference between the two prices.

As you can see, there are real life consequences and costs for failing to complete, which is why the fall-through rate at auctions represent a far lower rate comparatively than the fall-through rates in the market as a whole.

TRANSACTIONAL TRANSPARENCY

Why is transparency such an important element of the auction process? In the first instance, I would say that transparency brings certain types of sellers to the market:

1 **Institutional sellers:** Banks and building societies, local authorities, housing associations, receivers and administrators, central government and pension funds.

2 **Circumstance sellers:** Probate companies, estate executors (under probate), holders of lasting power of attorney and the official solicitor.

The transparent value of the auction for the above sellers offers them a credible and often crucial response to claims from shareholders/stakeholders/creditors/beneficiaries that the property was sold at under value. The true value of the auction is not measured against a perceived market value, but in most cases creates a true market value, based on the sales price of a property in an open and unfettered environment on the day of the auction.

When you see that a property has sold prior to the auction, I can almost certainly say that the property sold was not being offered by one of the above examples of seller. Transparency is one reason, if not *the* reason why they have decided to enter the property into the auction. The similar or secondary reason is to try and realise the best value for the property, which is backed up by the competitive nature and environment on the day of the auction.

CREATIVE PROPERTY OPPORTUNITIES

If you have a property that does not fall within the norm and requires a more considered approach, or indeed if there is a tangible or legal issue affecting the property, the estate agency route probably isn't the best path to take. Putting a property like this into the auction will be maximising its exposure to the most appropriate buyers and sellers within the market. You would be looking to present your property in such a way to highlight not only the issue, but with more importance, how that issue has the propensity to create greater levels of profitability.

A buyer looking to access 'problem' or 'underachieving' properties, will almost always look to the auction as a first port of call. Indeed, many people will normally expect a property in the auction to have a problem of some sort. Whilst this isn't always true, it does mean that these intrepid investors are looking to access properties that will require either a little TLC, or a considered and knowledgeable approach to fixing or restricting the property to increase profitability short, mid or long term. Problem solving is profit generating.

Knowing where best to market your property will save time, cost and effort. Knowing your market will further reduce time, cost and effort. Furthermore, knowing how to access properties that fit your investment strategy (as a buyer) will also reduce time, cost and effort.

Being creative will enable you to access opportunities that others would shy away from. The auction offers a fantastic amount of variety and opportunity.

NO CHAIN, NO PAIN

This is for all those who have had their sales or purchases fall through because there has been a break in the chain. A chain is a series of properties whose sale is conditional upon the seller finding somewhere else to live. This also applies to the buyers involved, whose ability to purchase is predicated on their existing property being sold.

Offers on properties are made all the time where the seller's ability to sell is conditional on their ability to buy another property, and where the buyer's ability to buy is conditional upon their ability to sell an existing property. When this happens (and it happens quite frequently), the number of links in this chain can be as small as four or six, and in some circumstances, as many as twenty or even thirty-plus links in the chain.

Now imagine if one or two of these links were unable to perform (for whatever reason). It is possible for the chain to fall apart. This can be a very frustrating consequence of property transactions.

The benefit of the auction is that a property is offered to the market chain free. In addition, the buyers are almost always chain free or, indeed, property professionals, where the purchase isn't conditional on the sale of an existing property. This section is also relevant for the certainty of sale section above, but it goes some way to showing how the auction market differs from the agency market, and even more so, highlights a benefit to the auction process. It also explains the advent of owner/occupiers submitting their properties to the auction and why so many owner/occupiers are attending the auctions to buy.

TOP 5 TIPS

@the.auction.pro

1. Auctions provide a wide range of properties at lower than market value prices. If you know how to solve the problems that caused those properties to end up in the auction, you will end up making money by buying at the right price.

2. Low guide and reserve prices might seem attractive, but you always need to consider the costs of adding value.

3. Speed is the key in auctions – that is why many of the properties end up in the auction. Make sure you have everything set up on a personal level, to be able to focus on the property research and provide the speed that is required.

4. Make sure you have means to complete. Failing to complete can have far wider consequences than losing the deposit. You will be liable for the seller's costs of selling and also for the difference in price if the property subsequently sells for less money. It might be easier and cheaper to find a way to buy the property and sell it again yourself! Consider your options carefully with your solicitor.

5. Being creative in how you approach your property transactions can allow you to unlock massive value in certain auction properties. It pays to be creative or have a team around you that can support such creativity!

CHAPTER 3
IT'S FREE – SO WHAT ARE YOU WAITING FOR?

I think that there is a big disparity in knowledge and experience within the property industry in general, and this is something that affects us all in one way or another. Putting yourself in a position to gain access to free and available knowledge and experience is certainly worth the time and effort to access it.

ATTENDING THE AUCTION

@the.auction.pro Most of the auctions are public auctions and you can go and watch the bidding process freely. Attending the auctions will give you the ability to sense how things are done in the auction room, how people bid, how auctioneers are conducting the bidding and squeezing every penny from the bidders.

Sometimes people stop themselves from going because they think they have no money to start buying. When I started, I had no money of my own. As a matter of fact, I started going to auctions to meet potential investors, target buyers of certain types of properties and generally make connections. If you think about it, most of the people bidding in the auction have cash, or access to cash, and not all of them end up buying a property. It's fairly easy to identify who the underbidder was. They already have funds, they were ready to purchase something, so they are the perfect person to approach if you are looking for clients. Do not expect an excessively warm reception though!

There were also properties that I thought were good deals, and I was curious to see how they were going to perform at auction. Once I gained some initial experience and got more comfortable with what's possible and how auctions work, I started offering some interesting auction lots to my clients, helping them to see the potential, navigating them through the auction process and charging a fee for a successful purchase. There are certain important factors of working with clients which are beyond the scope of this book but it is something that will be covered in the content on our site: www.beforethehammerfalls.co.uk.

Before you attend the auction, it is a good idea to go through the online version of the auction catalogue and review the properties that are being offered. Some of them will be particularly interesting. Highlight them and start doing online research as if you were going to purchase them. Review the comparable properties, google the full address including postcode, perhaps check EI Group portal (www.eigpropertyauctions.co.uk) for the previous auction sales, check out recent sales on the street and within a quarter or half a mile of the property.

@the.auction.insider All parts of this chapter are of equal importance and should be considered as such.

There really is nothing like the auction day. I say this whilst wearing the following hats – as a buyer, as a seller and as an auction professional.

1   As a buyer, I find myself in a perpetual heightened state of awareness whilst I am at the auction. It somehow magnifies once the lot I am interested in goes under the hammer. I tend to find a good spot in the room where I can have a mainly clear and unobstructed view of the room and other potential bidders. I am normally reluctant to stay in one place; I like to tell myself that there is a tactical purpose for moving around, but I think it comes down to the adrenaline.

2   As a seller, I take on a similar state to when I am in the auction looking to buy. There are subtle differences however. I normally start at the back of the room and tend to zero in on the bidders in the room. I think it provides me with a small degree of comfort when a bidder raises their hand or nods, thereby placing their bids. I am normally quite tense on the day anyway, but I find myself almost holding my breath until the bidding passes my reserve price.

3   My role on auction day is accidentally designed to be full of 'what could go wrong, will go wrong'. The day is structured and the processes at the contracts desk are clear and easy to action. That all falls to pieces when the winning bidder arrives. I have experienced the following on a regular basis:

   i   A winning bidder without identification. After new rules were brought in by HMRC in August 2017, the buyer must provide identification for the purposes of anti-money laundering requirements. These rules change regularly, so please make sure you have checked what is required in the first instance to avoid any mess and additional stress at the contracts desk.

ii   A winning bidder without their exchange deposit (or without an acceptable method to pay their deposit). This is possibly one of the scariest things to see and the most avoidable. Each auction house is likely to accept most forms or methods of payment and will normally list these in the notice to bidders well in advance of the auction. Not having the deposit available on the day of the auction instantly places you in breach of the contract. This is not a fun way to buy at auction.

iii A winning bidder has not read the legal pack. Although there is no requirement to read the legal pack, I find myself suppressing the most incredulous look I am capable of. It strikes fear in my heart. Do not be this person (pretty please).

There is more to the auction than just buying or selling property. It is arguably one of the best and most active environments for networking. It is full of action, enterprise and opportunity. An example of this (my go-to, when I miss out on an opportunity) is when I am outbid at the auction. I will wait for the auctioneer to approach the winning bidder (and myself as the underbidder) to take our details and then escort the winner to the contracts desk. I will then approach and introduce myself as the underbidder and offer my congratulations. I will also ask them what they plan on doing with the property and wish them well.

This is an important step for two reasons:

1   I am naturally quite nosy, but knowing what they plan to do can give me some idea as to why they had placed a higher value on the property than I had. It is a really useful exercise and most buyers are normally willing to share.

2   The winning bidder was looking at the same property in the same area and generally offered a bid at a value similar to you. The Joint Venture opportunity for the future is clearly there, and if not, it is certainly worth making contact and following up for a coffee.

ATTENDING THE VIEWINGS

@the.auction.pro Most of the auction properties have scheduled viewing times where you can go and inspect the property. There are a lot of lessons to learn while conducting viewings. When you see a very cheap property, it is only at the viewing that you might realise why it is so cheap.

If you are not an experienced builder, take one with you. You can always see more with two pairs of eyes, especially if you look at the property from different angles.

Have a rough idea of the end value of the property once you've purchased it and added value. Then use the spreadsheets to deduct all the necessary purchase and refurbishment costs. You will come up with a rough estimate of your maximum bid for that property. Compare it with the guide price of the property and check what it sells for afterwards.

This is the best way of learning about the auction process and also learning to detach yourself emotionally from the purchase. You come up with a figure, do the research and watch the process. At the end of it, you will see whether you would have won the bidding or not, but the most important lesson is that if you follow this process, you will eventually end up with a deal. If you want to end up with a deal too desperately, the auction is designed in such way that you can easily offer too much, and in effect win the bidding. But winning the bidding is only good if you won it at a reasonable price!

@the.auction.insider I cannot stress enough the importance of viewing the property in advance of the auction. I will go one further and say that if there are multiple viewings of the property, you should attend each viewing without exception. It may on the face of it sound like a total waste of your time – you know you've seen inside the property and not much is likely to change from one viewing to another.

I would suggest otherwise; there is one vital and normally unmeasurable variable in the calculation – the other attendees. I will point out that each attendee has the potential to become a bidder in the room. How valuable would it be for you to be able to recognise your potential competition on the day of the auction? This can make the difference between winning the property or walking away empty-handed.

Finally, go prepared and don't be shy – property is an investment after all and will involve the application of your hard-earned money. Here are a few suggestions for viewing a property:

1   **Come armed for any obstacle with a torch:** Not all properties will have an electrical supply, or may have it switched off in the case of repossessions and probates. Stepladder (I normally keep a collapsible one in the boot of my car) – perfect for looking at the nooks and crannies, and if a loft conversion is down as one of your added value exits, a step ladder is an absolute must. A cheap and cheerful laser measurer (or a smartphone application which allows you to create and measure floor plans) is also useful. There are some fairly cheap (worth the investment) damp sensors – useful not just for the bathroom, but surrounding rooms as well.

2   **You do not have to go alone.** I like to take someone with me to the second viewing that I attend. I attend the first viewing alone so as not to impact my initial thought process. Then I ask for an opinion for the second viewing. I think of this as obtaining a balanced and independent view, with the added potential bonus of that person spotting something I hadn't noticed (positive or negative, they are worth the same to me). Good recommendations for a viewing buddy (the second viewing) are friends and family (though not financially dependent family members). For the third viewing, I would recommend a property professional or

connected services professional. This can include builders, surveyors, an estate agent and maybe even an architect.

It is important to remember that you are not viewing the property just so you can tick it off your list of things to do. It is an important and potentially decisive element to purchasing a property at auction.

DOWNLOAD THE LEGAL PACK

@the.auction.insider I will discuss the legal pack in far more depth in other chapters, so will touch on its importance within this chapter in relation to its general importance and its accessibility.

A legal pack will always require the attention of a solicitor. I have yet to be swayed on this point. I would, however, recommend that you (the person making the decision, paying the deposit and of course living with your decision) download and read the legal pack for yourself. The power of self-education and building up knowledge about what is in a legal pack, what isn't in a legal pack and, of course, what different things mean is, for me, an absolute must.

Having access to this free information and experience and not taking the opportunity to have it enrich you in some way feels a little wasteful. A brilliant side effect of reading the legal pack is that you will suddenly have a greater understanding of the advice your solicitor provides you with, and you obtain a little more intimate knowledge of the property in the meantime.

An additional benefit is that you learn to get a feel for what is, in general terms, normal or abnormal within a legal pack and, hopefully, that will build a priceless sixth sense when it comes to evaluating the merits of purchasing a property or not.

This is purely the application of time and effort over adding value to yourself and your potential future purchases.

@the.auction.pro Legal packs are normally free to download for all the auction properties. They provide a lot of useful information on the property. Reviewing legal packs is important because it gives you a perspective on the property that you cannot get just from looking at the auction catalogue.

To download the legal pack, all you need to do is to register at the auctioneer's website. Most of the legal packs are available within the Auction Passport system which allows you to have one username for most auctions.

More on the legal packs in Chapter 9.

ONLINE RESEARCH

@the.auction.insider Just as with the legal pack section above, I will address this matter in far more detail in my section on due diligence, so will just expand on research in general terms and highlight the free avenues to online research which are invaluable when buying a property (and not just buying a property at auction).

A good starting point is to search the property address on the internet. I start with Google, but I do like some of the features of Bing such as the ability to draw out a site area and measure it. You are welcome to find your preference. I take this one step further by looking at the street view and locating the property. I'm not sure how many people know this, but it is worth mentioning – Google and Bing are constantly updating their maps, so in some instances, you can scroll back to two or even three different street views of the same road over the last couple of years. Google is very good for this and even date stamps when the picture was taken.

I then take a look at what is on the local market. This includes the online property portals (Rightmove and Zoopla to name but two), and I make a concerted effort to approach local agents, either on their website or over the phone because I like to engage with people and really get a feel for the local market.

There are of course other free and online sources to look at and perhaps add to your list of things to do before proceeding seriously with a property. In that regard, I would recommend creating a Net House Price account online; it is free and very easy to use. The site does not estimate the value of a property but advises on the marketing and sold prices of properties including the number of bedrooms – a very useful resource indeed.

With regards to Rightmove, I would recommend creating postcode alerts for areas of specific interest. The initial work involved in setting this up is well worth the value (although it can clog up your emails – but there are far worse things in life). I try and steer clear of property estimates as they are normally massive generalisations and can prove quite misleading if not approached with caution and a couple of pinches of salt.

I have recently started to use a website called 'In Your Area'. This has really revolutionised my due diligence process and allows me to have a bird's eye view over a specific area, which is vitally important, especially in cases where I am either not local to the area in question or have not purchased in the area previously. This is well worth a look and there is certainly no harm in adding it to your due diligence process. After all, it's free.

@the.auction.pro There are a variety of online tools that can be used for conducting online market research.

Online research is very important for me. We live in an age where a vast amount of information is available online and almost everything can be checked if you have access to the internet. I normally don't even attend a viewing before I am satisfied that there is no adverse information on the property online. This saves me thousands of pounds in time, travel costs and my own personal satisfaction, i.e. when I find that an attractive-looking property was offered several times in the auction at a very similar price and it went unsold. Online research usually then leads to some discoveries as to why that was the case. Viewing such properties would lead to a waste of time and resources that would be better deployed in finding a reason for failed sales.

FACEBOOK

@the.auction.insider Facebook has grown well beyond a photo and status sharing platform. Facebook has replaced a lot of the forums that used to be popular in the earlier days of the internet. There are a lot of property-related groups available for you to join for free. They all have a different audience and admins who specialise in a particular property field.

You can find all the links on the book's website – www. beforethehammerfalls.co.uk.

TELEVISION

It would be negligent not to mention the long-standing BBC television show *Homes Under the Hammer*. There are hundreds of people every year who approach the auctions and buy from the auction because of their interaction with *Homes Under the Hammer*. It takes viewers on a journey with the purchaser and shows you from an independent point of view what happens at the auction. It is certainly worth watching a couple of episodes, as I think this will help to prepare you for the auction day and purchasing environment.

TOP 5 TIPS

@the.auction.pro

1 You don't need money to start being active in auctions. Auctions are a goldmine for potential clients who have money available to purchase or do business with.

2 Choose a spot in the auction room that will give you good visibility and control over what is happening in the room. It's probably best to avoid front rows for that reason, although if you are bidding, do also make sure you are visible to the auctioneer.

3 Browsing through freely provided legal packs can give you a lot of insight into properties and it's a good starting point.

4 After you have looked at some legal packs and done some basic online research, view the properties and get a feel for the property and the area.

5 TV programmes about buying in auction are a valuable source of inspiration. However, they tend to miss a lot that really goes into a deal so probably best to use common sense before accepting all the conclusions from the programme.

CHAPTER 4
IT'LL COST YOU – BUT NOT AS MUCH AS YOU MIGHT THINK

@the.auction.insider In the last chapter, we discussed a couple of the free and easily accessible resources available to you. In this chapter, I am going to discuss those resources available to you, but at a price.

@the.auction.pro There is a variety of paid subscription portals, property networking meetings and tools that a property investor can use to enhance the due diligence process, make it simpler and also obtain the knowledge and contacts necessary to make the property business successful. Below is a list of various paid tools that I am using and how I use them.

It's important to pick those that are going to be valuable to you for the specific purpose that you need them. It's easy for all the memberships and subscriptions to add up to several hundred pounds a month, so you should choose wisely what you are going to need.

MONTHLY PROPERTY MEETS

@the.auction.pro I have benefited enormously from attending property networking meetings. Since about 2013, I have regularly attended property investors' meetings in London.

Through those meetings I have made various business contacts – Joint Venture (JV) partners whom I have done deals with, clients to whom I have offered my property services, investors who have invested funds in my projects, solicitors, architects, accountants and other professionals that have acted for my company. When attending and meeting new people at the networking meetings, it's important to carry out due diligence on anyone who you are considering doing business with. These meets are very friendly and supportive, but it's important to always use common sense and your intuition when it comes to engaging in business with others. I'd suggest speaking with at least three other people who have used, are using services or are doing business with the person with whom you would like to engage. It's also good to ask the opinion of the event host as they are likely to know people in the room.

There are several property meetings that you can find near you:

PROPERTY INVESTORS NETWORK (pin) MEETINGS

There are about fifty pin meetings around the UK, set up by Simon Zutshi. Simon is a property investor and probably one of the most recognised property educators in the UK. I have trained with Simon and I was one of the top five performers on the twelve-month Property Mastermind Programme run by him. A big part of the Mastermind Programme is networking and attending pin meetings.

pin meetings are always in the evenings from 6 p.m. to 9 p.m. with the main part of the evening starting at 7 p.m. It's worth adding that the networking usually continues beyond 9 p.m. in the bar and it's as valuable as the meeting itself.

The pin meetings cost £20 per meeting. If you have never attended a pin meeting before, you can come as my guest and save yourself £20 by using the voucher code 'Piotr' at the checkout.

If you like pin meetings and would like to attend them regularly, it might be worth considering signing up for the pin academy, which combines education with online support for property investors who are looking to educate themselves. Subscription costs £40 +VAT per month and it includes unlimited access to pin meetings around the country. So, if you are attending two pin meetings a month, your cost would pretty much be recouped. You can even trial it for one month for £1. For more info on pin Academy, go to https://www.pinacademy. co.uk/pin-academy-special/.

PROGRESSIVE PROPERTY NETWORK (PPN) MEETINGS

Another large network of property meetings is the Progressive Property Network, which has meetings all over the country. Those meetings tend to attract a slightly different crowd to pin meetings (although there is a lot of crossover) so it's worth exploring those too. For more information on your local meet visit: https:// progressivepropertynetwork.co.uk/find-your-local-ppn/.

INDEPENDENT MEETS

There are a lot of independently-run property meetings in London and the rest of the country. They might have a different format to pin or PPN meetings and also a different flavour, as it is all down to the host to choose the way they are run.

You might want to check Your Property Network (YPN) Magazine and Property Investors News (PIN) for up-to-date information on most of the property meetings.

@the.auction.insider This is a big part of my personal and professional life. The cost of the meets is fairly negligible (and even more so if you take out a membership). Almost all of the meets I have attended offer a lot of value and extras if you commit to an annual membership. Even so, it is certainly worth employing the 'try before you buy' approach. For the following reasons, and at the very least:

1   I would recommend attending the meet or meets you are looking at investing in (annual membership) at least twice before taking the plunge. It gives you an idea of the type of people attending, the content of the meets and, most importantly, the networking opportunity (which for me remains one of the most important reasons to attend).

2   I would recommend more than one annual membership. It is important that you are a member at the right event and employing your time and money effectively. To this effect, I would suggest one London (or major city) event and one local or independent property meet.

There are plenty of options out there and each of them offers something special. It is worth noting that the people who run the meets normally have a specialism, so I would take this into consideration and potentially align myself with that meet to obtain more knowledge in that area (if that was part of my investment strategy).

ESSENTIAL INFORMATION GROUP (EIG)

I would say that I use the EIG software on a daily basis, despite having had little interaction with it prior to becoming an auction professional. I try not to think too much about that, because I imagine I'd be kicking myself about all the missed information and opportunities as a result.

I use this software mainly for two purposes, one which is almost exclusively for the auction professional, and one which is available to all for an annual unlimited use fee.

1 The auction professional will use the EIG group system in one of two different ways. The first being the use of their catalogue creation software (DMS) and secondly their legal pack storage and access system (Auction Passport). We use the latter to check whether a legal pack has been uploaded to the system via the seller's solicitor and secondly, how many people have interacted with the legal pack.

2 EIG is first and foremost a living historical and current record of all properties entered to auction. You can set up auction alerts and even use the system to find comparable evidence for similar properties. This is important, because it will provide you with the auction result and not the open

market value result. This will show you the difference between your maximum bid price (or an indication at the very least) and the potential market value.

It is worth engaging with their system if you are looking to approach the auction market regularly and seriously. At the time of writing this book, I know that they have been offering a trial period before you fully commit to their annual subscription. So it's worth making contact for the trial at the very least.

MASTERCLASSES

I think that it is highly important to ensure that you are constantly learning and improving. The property market by its very nature is a market of constant change. There can be yearly changes to practice, procedure, law and regulation. Making sure that you are up-to-date with the changes within the industry is vitally important; you do not want to be operating on old or even defunct knowledge.

I believe that recent legislative changes which relate specifically to how landlords' businesses are structured are part of increasing the professionalism and overall public opinion of landlords in general.

How to know when changes such as these are coming, how to adapt to those changes and how to put best practice in place can make the difference between a successful property business and an unsuccessful one.

Solicitors and accountants are expected to enlist in post-qualification experience: there are normally requirements to get a certain amount of points per annum to make sure that your knowledge and understanding are up-to-date. I believe that the property professional should endeavour to do the same. This can include personal and professional development.

A masterclass or equivalent course in your selected property subject, especially close to a paradigm-shifting event in the industry is seriously worth the time and effort. This applies equally to the beginner, the emerging professional and the master in the trade.

There are several masterclasses available throughout the UK; there are some very generic courses on property in general terms and these are a good starting point for most. Additionally, there are some quite specific courses (e.g. covering listed property conversions, permitted development and HMOs).

The majority of these masterclasses can be accessed via the property networking scene, most of which are offered by the hosts of the events and indeed, some of the specialist speakers.

@the.auction.pro Before I started networking and educating myself by going to property courses, I was working as a sourcing agent. This gave me the knowledge of properties, the basic confidence to negotiate some deals and experience on how to make money in property. However, this was all from the perspective of an agent. This is how other people saw me and how I saw myself. It was difficult to find JV partners. The breakthrough came when I joined the twelve-month

Mastermind Programme with Simon Zutshi. The fears and uncertainties were still there but I knew that I had around me a group of fifty people, all of whom were willing to contribute with complementary skills or resources. Some people can provide the legwork, some come with years of experience, some have access to cash. But no-one really has all of this and in the group environment, people are willing to trade the rewards for the complementary skills.

The same happens when attending masterclasses or short courses. For me, the benefit of a long-term programme is the commitment that it creates. With short courses and masterclasses, you will need to ensure that you put some structures in place so that you continue using the information that you learned.

When choosing the courses, you should pick reputable trainers and partners. Feel free to reach out to Facebook property groups and ask people about their experiences with a particular trainer.

SEE WHAT THE PROFESSIONALS SEE

@the.auction.insider Access to the invisible world of the property market isn't as hard as you might at first think. In the early days, in order to access this part of the market you would need to be an estate agent or equivalent, which put quite a high bar on access for most. With the advent of corporatisation (incorporating your properties under a limited company, for instance) most investors, developers and generally sellers (best for property traders) can access this invisible market area:

1 **Rightmove+ (plus):** Rightmove plus is the record of all properties marketed by Rightmove. That doesn't sound very impressive on the face of it, but here's the kicker – it has all properties sold, unsold, archived, withdrawn from the market, everything. Imagine this; you are looking at a property on a specific road, you go on to Rightmove to see what is currently on the market – but the information is limited, and you want a better idea of the transactional history of the road. Rightmove plus gives you this, can build reports and in some circumstances, can show you the price paid and the date the price was paid (via the Land Registry).

2 **Zoopla Pro:** Zoopla Pro is the Zoopla equivalent to Rightmove+. Generally speaking, it offers a similar service, but it can be argued that the reporting element is a little easier to navigate and, in some instances, can provide more information than that of the Rightmove+ offering. I am speaking about both offerings not to draw too much of a comparison, but to highlight what the benefits of potentially having these services can add to your business. Rightmove still holds the majority of the market share, but that does not mean that you should instantly dismiss Zoopla Pro.

3 **Essential Information Group (EIG):** Although I have discussed this above, it is worth highlighting a different element. When you are looking at a property at auction, it may be that the property has been at auction previously

(not on Rightmove or Zoopla) or indeed the nearest comparable property had been offered via auction – the best and most reliable way to access this information would be with an EIG account. This can really make a difference to your purchase of a property and furthermore the price at which you purchase.

4   **LonRes:** This is a little specific and potentially may not apply across the board, but certainly worth discussing. It does relate specifically to the London property market, so if investing in the London property market is a large part of your investment strategy (residential), it's very useful. This is a great tool, which takes some of the best bits of Rightmove+ and Zoopla Pro and makes that information far more accessible. The data archives are well-maintained and contain some very useful data points.

5   **CoStar:** I admit that up to about two years ago I was wholly unaware of CoStar. Now I know about them, my life (insofar as commercial property is concerned) has certainly changed. What makes them different, is that they manually update their results and information directly with the agent/seller. This, I feel, makes their results a little more reliable. There are many other benefits to their service, including market updates, newsletters and blogs. This is a must-have addition to your property journey, if commercial (mixed use) property is part of your investment strategy.

TOP 5 TIPS

@the.auction.pro

1 Investing in your education is the key to success.

2 Through courses and property meets, you will be expanding your network and net worth.

3 Having access to the right resources such as eigpropertyauctions.co.uk, known as the Rightmove of auction properties, will give you a head start with your due diligence and access to quality information.

4 Paid subscriptions to property magazines such as Property Investor News, Estates Gazette and others, are a phenomenal source of up-to-date market commentary and case studies. This adds to your existing knowledge base.

5 Applying what you have learned is essential in producing results.

CHAPTER 5
KNOWING WHAT'S IMPORTANT – INFORMATION PROVIDED PRIOR TO THE AUCTION

@the.auction.insider A property entered to auction will have information provided at different stages of the process leading up to the auction day. It can be a very information-heavy process (not including your own due diligence/ fact-finding exercises) which starts with the entry into the auction catalogue.

Between the printing of the catalogue and the auction day, a lot can change. Below is an indicative timeline of a property's journey from creation of the catalogue entry to the auction day and the exchange of contracts.

THE CATALOGUE

The catalogue never feels like it is enough, but at the same time I cannot foresee a time in the near future where the physical catalogue will not be printed. There is something quite reassuring and tactile to have a catalogue with you on the day of the auction (either to use to bid or to hide your emotions from the other bidders). The information is normally basic and the number of pictures that can be printed on a single entry can be quite restrictive. Fortunately, the primary functions of the auction catalogue are to:

1   Expose the property to the market.

2   Highlight key features and basic information.

3   Disclose the guide price.

4   Show any income information.

5   Show any planning permission.

In short, it is the purpose of the auction catalogue to give you a brief insight (at a glance) into the property, prompting interest and further investigation. (Insider tip: do not bid for a property at auction based solely on the contents of the catalogue entry.)

THE WEBSITE

If your sole approach to the auction is to register for the catalogue and the legal pack, please consider adding the following actions to your auction interactions:

1   Additional pictures (internal and external).

2   Floor plans (with or without internal measurements).

3   Site plans, proposed floor plans and elevations (entries with planning permission).

4   Viewing times/additional viewing times.

5   Checking the status of the property (sold prior to the auction, withdrawn from the auction or postponed to a future auction).

6   Checking to see if there are any late entries.

7   The addendum (if there is one).

I always recommend looking at the auctioneer's website. You never know what you might miss out on by just relying on the catalogue.

THE LEGAL PACK

Your ability to purchase a property at auction will be greatly affected or influenced by the presence of contents, or the lack of contents, that are provided within the legal pack. In short, the legal pack is provided in advance of the auction (at any stage prior to the start of the auction).

I consider the legal pack and the addendum two of the most important sources of information provided by the sellers and the auctioneers. It is important to remember that a decision to buy cannot be made solely upon the details contained within the catalogue, website, legal pack or addendum. These sources are no substitute for a robust programme of due diligence.

All the above, and indeed the remainder of the chapter, should form part of your due diligence, but cannot be the only elements of your diligence practices.

The legal pack can be available from the point of instruction, or earlier, as is the case with corporate sellers (bank sales, receivership sales, local authority sales etc.) and all the way up to the start of the auction, but no later. There is of course an optimal time for the legal pack to be available and, in my opinion, the legal pack should be available on the day of the second viewing.

My reasoning for this is that most investors are likely to view the property on at least two occasions prior to the auction. You can capitalise on this by ensuring that before or just after that second viewing (but on the same day) they are notified of the legal pack's availability. It is important to enable a purchaser to view and conduct their due diligence on the property in question.

For the benefit of both the seller and any of the interested parties, the early disclosure of the legal pack can achieve the following:

1   It can increase bidder confidence when making preparations to attend the auction and bid.
2   It allows the interested parties to carry out further due diligence in advance of the auction.
3   It allows you to highlight any potential issues with the property that are not apparent in the first instance.
4   It can increase the number of pre-auction offers you can make as a buyer and receive as a seller.

In a later chapter, we will be discussing the legal pack and its contents in far greater detail.

THE ADDENDUM

This is one of the most overlooked sources of information provided prior to the exchange of contracts. The addendum refers to an in-life change, which means a change in the property that has been disclosed or realised after the printing of the catalogue.

The addendum will also notify you of any properties that have been sold or withdrawn prior to the auction, or postponed to a future auction. The addendum will also highlight any changes from the norm. This can include the deposit amount (which is usually 10 per cent), the buyer's fee amount, or the addition of a buyer's premium. It can also stipulate an appropriate form of deposit (e.g. no cheques, or cleared funds only).

The addendum can be issued in the following ways:

1   The addendum is available on the auctioneer's website, sometimes as a downloadable PDF, or as part of that property's online auction entry.
2   There will also be a printed version made available on the day of the auction, which is another reason to make sure that you attend the auction on time.
3   Additionally, it is customary for the auctioneer to read through the addendum at the start of the auction and relay that same information when introducing the property prior to bidding.
4   Finally, there may be a verbal addendum which is equally as binding as the written addendum and again this will be disclosed by the auctioneer, prior to the commencement of bidding for that specific property.

Remember that the addendum supersedes all other information provided (the catalogue, the website and the legal pack).

Not being aware of the addendum means that you may either miss out on a vitally important piece of information which is beneficial to that property, and decide not to bid because you did not have the information available, or that you have missed out on a piece of information which detrimentally affects your ability to purchase, or interferes directly with your investment strategy.

TOP 5 TIPS

@the.auction.pro

1 Do not ever rely solely on the catalogue entry. The information there might not be 100 per cent accurate and, after printing, the information might be corrected via addendum. Check if your property is there. Use the catalogue as high-level information that requires verification in official documents.

2 Past catalogue entries are a useful source of information. Many past catalogues can be accessed on the EIG website, or by googling the address of the property with 'filetype:pdf' included in the search.

3 The auctioneer's website will normally have more up-to-date and more thorough information on property than the printed catalogue, as the website can be constantly updated when new information comes to light.

4 Always register for the legal pack updates for the property you are interested in. It's not enough to just download it once, as it can be altered or updated at any time before the

auction. Always ensure you read the latest additions to the legal pack.

5 An addendum can be verbal and announced right before your lot is being offered. Listen carefully to what the auctioneer says before opening the bidding.

CHAPTER 6
DECIDING ON WHAT'S RIGHT FOR YOU

@the.auction.insider In this chapter, we will be looking at how to maintain your investment strategy by looking at your exit strategy and building a property journey to avoid getting lost along the way. There is some bonus material at the end of the book which goes into greater detail on an exit strategy. For now, we will look at it as a principle and why it requires so much consideration.

I do not want to make this chapter too philosophical, but when discussing some of the sections below, we may take a trip into the 'meaning of life' area.

WHAT IS YOUR WHY?

Maybe it's best to get the philosophical bits out of the way first, and then get back to the rest of the chapter once we've looked at ourselves first.

'He who has why can endure any how.'
– Friedrich Nietzsche

I personally have spent a lot of time trying to figure out my why and the looking at how I am going to achieve it. There are a lot of resources online and there are a lot of people talking about finding your purpose, 'finding your why'. I have tried to narrow it down to four questions you can ask yourself (in the examples below it is property-centric, but feel free to use it in other areas of life).

1   **What are your core values?** This is something that dictates pretty much every decision we make in life. Your core values can be based on your religious teachings, the lessons taught to you by parents/friends/mentors; your values could be based on your environment and can be the sum of your experiences, the good and the bad. What is important is that you align your core values with your WHY – this must come from you, and to achieve it, you must be able to act it out in accordance with your own values at the heart of it.

2   **What are you passionate about?** This is something that drives you forward, that fire in your belly that gives you the power and the energy to achieve. For me, passion without focus is loss. If you can take that drive and energy and align it with your WHY, it means that you have introduced focus to your passion and can put those energies to effective use.

3   **What natural talents do you have (your strength)?** This is any strength or talent that you find comes naturally to you, something which is almost effortless, or is so innate within you that you do it naturally without even realising it. One of the best ways to realising your why, or putting you on the path to realising your why and achieving your why, is

to implement that one strength or talent to help you excel with achieving your WHY – it means that from the off, you are able to rely on that one talent, your greatest strength, to realise your goal.

4   **What is your primary skill set (your expertise)?** This is the area that enables you to add the most value to your why and to yourself. Your expertise doesn't have to be property based; it can be a financial background, it can be a project management background – it can be pretty much any background, so long as you are willing to look at the expertise you have gained and apply it to your WHY – it means that every skill is transferable and that in putting your why into action, you are also taking what skills you have with you to help you learn new skills along the way.

At this point in the chapter, I bet you are asking yourself why I have put you through all the above. Well, that's simple – WHY? is the best question you can ask yourself at any point in your property journey; indeed, when looking at any property to buy and equally so when looking to sell your property.

Here are a few examples:

1   Why is the vendor selling and why have they chosen the auction to do so?
2   Why does that property look so cheap?
3   Why are there no searches in the legal pack?
4   Why are there no viewings?
5   Why is there no floor plan?

It is important to know the why, and the why is the reason you are looking to buy and/or sell through auctions. It is why you are looking to invest in property over stocks and shares, for instance. At the heart of it all, you are looking to achieve something and perhaps property is just one of the means you employ in getting there.

Maybe your why is financial freedom, building a pension pot, wanting to make a difference to people's standards of living, creating a property empire for your children and their children; whatever it is, it has to be at the heart of what you do to make it a success – and more importantly, to make sure you don't get lost along the way. The why will determine more of your investment strategy than you may first think, so it is worth a taking little time at the outset to make sure that you know what you are going to be doing and why.

ARE YOU TRENDY?

I don't think I have ever been trendy. I've either been too far ahead of the curve or too far behind it to be classed as trendy (certainly not a trendsetter). Then again, I have an investment strategy which must be about a hundred years old. What makes my investment strategy different from a hundred years ago, or from anyone else using the same strategy, is me – I am what makes the difference.

It is exactly the same with you, wonderful reader (whoever you may be). You are what makes the difference with any investment strategy you choose. I have provided a few examples of current (or trendy) investment strategies below:

1 Property development (incl. modular developments).
2 Houses in Multiple Occupation (HMO).
3 Service accommodation.
4 Commercial property.
5 Single let.
6 Sub-dividing & title splits.
7 Land banking.
8 Planning gain (new-build & existing property).

The list really could go on forever, but I have kept it short otherwise I could really get carried away.

Do not be afraid to do what others are doing and equally do not be afraid to do your own thing. Property is diverse and has many applications. Pick the one that's right for you and play to your strengths.

THE CRYSTAL BALL OF OPPORTUNITY

There are some amazing people out there in the property world who spend a lot of their time and effort looking at the property market (and the external factors: domestic and international politics, banking and finance and the legislature, to name a few) to decide where and what they are going to invest in next.

This can range from spreadsheets and diagrams all the way down to looking back over the last twenty-five to fifty years and divining a property cycle, measuring the ups and the downs, and those little indicators that usher in one or the other.

I think that when you are looking at investing in a new market or investing for the first time, there are things you should consider and that should form part of your research before you even spend a penny:

1. Take advantage of as much free information as you possibly can. Whether it be changes to a bank's lending criteria, or changes in the law that affect landlords – all the way over to the changes in the House Price Index or the departure of Britain from the European Union. All these things will have an impact. I like to look at the Office of National Statistics (ONS) – they do a lot of the research for you. Whilst I may not always agree with their conclusion, I will always take their statistics and analyse that information for myself.
2. Your investment strategy is likely to start (or to have started off) quite small and simple (the same way we all start). This normally means that you will get to focus on a specific type of investment in a specific area.

CORE INVESTMENT AREA

There are a lot of benefits to investing in an area that you are familiar with, or know, or have known for many years. It is a prudent investment strategy to do so. I know that a lot of investors start in their 'comfort zone' and some very successful investors will normally stay within a relatively short distance of their core investment area, 'the ground zero'. Let's face it, the reduced cost and ease of managing all your investments within a small locale offers significant benefits. The following sources of information can offer you remote insights into another area, thereby enabling you to increase your investment catchment.

1 **It starts with the postcode:** I like to google the postcode, zoom out and have a good look at the specific area and the general location. I pay close attention to the local schools, public transport and accessibility ('A' roads and 'M' roads, where they lead from and where they lead to). I like to look at the street view of the town/city centre as this allows me to see what kind of amenities are nearby and gives me an idea of the local population demographic.

2 **Postcode profile:** Continuing on from the postcode search, I find great insight and value by using UK Local Area (uklocalarea.com) and likewise with In Your Area (inyourarea.co.uk). This is the step above and beyond. It can take what you have seen on Google and Google street view and create a report. It will detail census statistics (not always the most recent, but a good indicator), house prices, school results, council tax banding, energy prices, local transportation information and street-level crime (powered by police.uk).

3 **The local authority is an authority on the locale:** A frequently missed fountain of information is the local council website. Anything from local community projects and notices, through to planning applications, can really

give you an insider's feel for the area. I try to take advantage of the planning portal – a public platform to look at all the properties in the road, or surrounding roads that you are looking at. Seeing what has been approved, what has been refused and what is proceeding to appeal can really help you decide on what kind of added value you can create, roughly how long it might take and how much it could cost. For me, this is an extremely valuable source of free and accessible information.

THE LOCAL MARKET

As discussed previously, and in one of the bonus chapters, it is advisable to take advantage of as much free information as is humanly possible. The use of Rightmove, Zoopla, Net House Price and Mouse Price should be considered a minimum standard as sources for your basic research.

It is important to consider adding the following to your list of sources when looking to highlight specific properties in line with your specific investment strategy:

1 **House Price Index (HPI):** This is a regular report available based on figures obtained directly from the Land Registry and is available publicly. The only downside or consideration to take when looking at this information is that it is generally two to three months behind the current day (the primary reason for this is that it can take up to three months for the Land Registry to update its records).

2   **Nationwide House Price Index (NHPI):** If, like me, you like to obtain a second opinion or indeed, just another point of view, then the Nationwide Building Society offers a back catalogue of HPI information which is free to access and download (the difference with the NHPI is that it is downloadable as an annual report, so the number can be a little diluted, but in conjunction with the HPI, it helps to create a more rounded picture).

3   **Net House Price & Mouse Price (mentioned above):** These provide a similar service to the HPI and NHPI, but with both of these additional services, you can select a specific postcode, draw a heat map of prices and set alerts for sold prices for a specific area, which will notify you of any significant increases or decreases in your investing area/s.

4   **Hometrack.com:** This is a treasure trove of information (if you are a data-driven person, that is). I like the following services/tools they offer: the UK Cities Index, the Market Intelligence tool and the Risk Analytics tool. It is worth noting that this is a paid service provider, unlike the other providers I have mentioned thus far, and I would recommend a demo for anyone looking to professionalise and systemise their property business.

When researching property in a specific area, you have the ability to track and record the changes down at a micro level. This will give a little insight into the changes in the market and, to a certain extent, the future of that market.

To supplement the above, I would recommend canvassing the local market. The starting point for me is to make contact with at least two estate agents (I prefer one of them to be an independent estate agency – the opinions can vary quite drastically, so it's good to get a well-rounded view).

THE FRONTLINE TROOPS – ESTATE AGENTS

I have not been an estate agent for approximately ten years, but I understand what it is to be an estate agent and what value an estate agent has to an investor. It is important, I feel, that when you do engage with an estate agent, you are making the most of it. The following are some of the questions I ask when I am looking at a property in an unfamiliar area with a local estate agent on the phone:

1 **Drop it like it's HOT**: What is hot in the local market at the moment/what is in demand? This is always my first question and it really helps me look at my prospective investment to see how much demand there is in the local area. You can expect to get a generic response back, so do not be afraid to dig a little deeper – if it's houses, how many bedrooms? Which roads are commanding the best prices? If it's flats, again, how many bedrooms, with or without parking and/or outside space?

2 **What's New?**: I like to know about changes in the local market, so I ask them if sales have increased over the last six months or so. Likewise, I ask what the lettings market

is like and how long it takes for a property to go under offer or to be let. I lead the question towards development, ask if there are any recently finished developments in the area, or anything exciting that has just started.

3   **The Who's Who**: If you take the time to utilise the free sources above, you are likely to have a good idea of the buyer/renter demographic. The numbers can sometimes be out of date or skewed in some cases, so engaging with a local specialist can really help to reinforce the data or bring clarity to it. Asking them about what type of people are buying tells you a lot, but the most important part for me is who is looking to rent in the local area. This tells me who (most likely) I'll be renting my property to or indeed, who may be renting the property next door. This can influence my fit and finish (costs) and even my purchase price to reflect a strong yield position.

4   **Fast Forward**: I like to structure a purchase and sale with a minimum of a six-month turnaround. I do this because I like to enable mortgage buyers to be in a position to exchange on my properties, and since they occupy the largest part of the market, I make a concerted effort to include them. This means I like to complete a purchase, have it rented on a six-month rental agreement and have it exchanged at the end of the agreement. I then serve notice to the tenant (depending on the buyer) with a notice that comfortably fits the completion and sell on (either tenanted or vacant). For this to work, I always ask what the estate agent thinks his market will look like in six months. I want

to know who's looking at the market at that time, if there is any capital appreciation and if my purchase is still going to be hot property.

I hope that the above highlights the importance of really looking at a local market (even more so when it is an unfamiliar market) in knowing where and when best to strike and what you can achieve. This all forms part of being able to highlight appropriate properties and take that one step further and buy. This I hope is a general rule but is vitally applicable to properties found at auction.

DECIDING ON WHAT'S RIGHT FOR YOU

@the.auction.pro The properties offered in the auction come with their own history and set of circumstances. It's very important that you understand how to highlight suitable properties for you to bid on so that you avoid getting overwhelmed by the number of properties in the catalogue. I review almost all the London auction's catalogues and the number of properties I look at can go into around 500–1000 a month. In this chapter, I'll share with you what I do to highlight suitable properties. The chapter will feature some considerations and then it will end with a process that will help you identify the right opportunities.

YOUR INVESTMENT STRATEGY

Your investment strategy is the most important aspect of choosing the right properties to bid on. You need to be crystal clear about what your investment strategy is and WHY you are looking to purchase properties. If you are looking to increase your cashflow, then you will be looking out for different properties than if you are looking for short-term capital gain or long-term capital growth. You may also be purchasing a property for strategic purposes. Maybe you already own a house next door and owning two will create opportunities that other people do not have access to, such as connecting the properties and building a block of flats.

So, what is the purpose of you purchasing the property? Spend some time thinking about this as it will affect everything. Purchasing property leads to consequences and responsibilities and consequently investing further resources in fulfilling those. If you choose to purchase property that does not suit your investment strategy, then you are committing to something that will not forward your goals and aspirations. So do not let the price of the property seduce you into buying or even attempting to buy something unsuitable.

Factors to consider when looking at investment strategy:

1 **Purpose:** Cashflow; short-term capital gain; long-term capital gain; strategic purchase.
2 **Type of purchase:** Ready-made investment or requires enhancing.

3   **Timeframe for exit:** Up to six months; twelve months; two years; five years; ten years; lifetime.

4   **Geography:** Area and radius from the property.

5   **Exit strategy:** Sell; hold; part-sell; part-hold.

WATCH OUT FOR BEING CARRIED AWAY BY TRENDS

You need to watch out for those types of hot properties that everyone is after. This could be, for example, office blocks (B1a use) that can be converted into residential properties (amongst many others). These types of properties were significantly less popular in 2012–2013 when there were not permitted development rights to convert them to residential without lengthy planning applications. Since then, lots of people have made a lot of money converting office blocks into flats and the demand for those have increased significantly to the extent that people tend to be overpaying for them. As with many properties, there might be very motivated buyers looking to purchase them. You should not try to outbid them. Stick to your game. Winning the bidding is only good if you are within your limits.

Usually the opportunities will lie in those properties that, for most of the buyers, are a liability. In recent years, with the growth of online shopping and Amazon, the retail shops and shopping centres tend to be getting empty. An empty commercial property can be a big liability for the owner, who would have to pay business rates on the property. Retail properties, traditionally purchased by people looking for safe returns, are now seen as risky investments. So there needs to be a new type of buyer to purchase those properties. If you can find a way of turning such a liability back into an asset that is producing income and making money, you are on to a goldmine – similar to investors who were early adopters of converting office buildings into residential flats under permitted development.

CASE STUDY

Shopping centres used to be extremely popular in the past and almost exclusively sold by private treaty to all sort of funds. With the increase of online shopping and the retail market struggling, shopping centres are more often disposed via auctions. One of our recent case studies was a shopping centre with a four-storey car park located in the centre of Falkirk, Scotland. It was offered in an Acuitus auction at a guide price of £1 million and income of over £620,000 per annum, but running at less than 40 per cent occupancy. There were, however, some large costs of running the space of about £600,000 per annum. So, the actual profit was only about £20,000 per annum! The costs of building such a centre would be around £15 million to £20 million so, in a sense, it was a bargain. But the sentiment in the market is to stay away from such centres as they become a liability. This opportunity was sensed by a couple of dynamic investors from London with a strong family backing. They bid on the property in the auction and won it at £1,005,000. However, they had a clear plan from the start on what to do with the space. On the day of the completion of the transaction, they organised a community party in the shopping centre, inviting locals to the start of the new future of the centre. Their vision of the shopping centre is to turn it into a community asset and a space for a lot of small, local independent shops to take advantage of the central location. This is going against the trend of purchasing retail, but going with the trend of community-inspired spaces and services. Always remember where in the trend-cycle you are in order to be able to deliver a successful project.

A full article from Estates Gazette on this case study can be accessed on our website under Chapter 6.

PAST EXPERIENCE AND LOCAL KNOWLEDGE

In many instances, if you have bought a property before, you will have a really good idea of the property values and the demand in the area. So will every other investor who has a property there, but none of them are reviewing catalogues, bidding on properties, or even being in a position to purchase at the same time that you are. So, you might find yourself having certain advantages over other people who are looking to bid on the property in the area of your interest. Some people call it your 'goldmine area'. Having local knowledge pays off in the auction, even if it only leads you to stop bidding on a certain property.

You might also have a past experience of bidding or trying to purchase a property in a given area. You will have had the benefit of hindsight of what happened with that property over time. Was it worth it? Did it do well?

CASE STUDY

In May 2014, about six months after I started Synergy Property Partners, there was a very attractive-looking pub offered in the auction. The guide price was £350,000+ which seemed unbelievably good value. The place was, however, very run-down and had some structural issues with the rear extension. I went to see it with an architect, in order to assess potential to convert or build a residential scheme there. The architect was very excited, as there was a large car park, suitable for a block of six flats and a further three flats in the main building. I quickly found out that we could underwrite this property at £420,000 which was still good value (more on underwriting in the Bonus Chapter 1). In the process of searching for an investor, the architect made calls to the planning department of the local council and learned that the council would be against turning the pub into a residential property. In fact, they had already refused a similar application from the current seller. The warning lights went off. We decided to stay away from the purchase. The property was then auctioned off and to my surprise the property sold for an eye-watering £735,000! If we had underwritten the property, we would have made 45 per cent of the difference between the underwriting price, £420,000 and the sale price of £735,000, i.e. £141,750! I was disappointed, but I knew we were missing vital information and could not afford the risk of things going wrong.

About a year later, to my surprise, the property appeared in another auction again. This time, with beautiful computer-generated images showing what a new development of eight *apartments and ground-floor pub would look like! It already had planning granted and the guide price was £1.5 million plus! Double the purchase price that had already been huge! The development had a gross development value (GDV) of about £3.5 million and is now fully completed. The learning for me from this was to look for multiple exits in every transaction. The next step will probably be converting the pub space into retail or office space. The upside in this transaction was great but we were focused solely on development instead of thinking about what else we could do with this should the development be refused!*

PROCESS OF HIGHLIGHTING SUITABLE PROPERTIES

I search auction catalogues for opportunities that either I or my clients could benefit from. So, my radar is fairly broad. In order to ensure I don't miss any good deals, I review auction catalogues several times, applying different filters to my search. I tend to follow the process described below.

1   **Very quick short-listing of the properties.** Scan the auction catalogue for something that you are intending to purchase, e.g. if I am looking for properties that can generate a short-term gain in capital value, I tend to highlight anything that remotely catches my attention and has potential for generating profit quickly. The properties that could fall into this category include short leases, unmodernised property in an area of interest, properties with potential to

extend, commercial properties that are vacant and would be suitable for residential conversion, commercial properties that are vacant and could be suitable for a good commercial tenant (such as Costa Coffee etc.), or existing houses split into multiple flats. All those properties have a potential for enhancing value and generating profit within a short period of time. So, they go on the initial short-list and are earmarked for further research. Don't worry if you pick lemons (at this stage it's better to choose too many than miss the potential diamond). Don't spend too much time reviewing each property either. If it catches attention for whatever reason, it goes onto the shortlist.

2   **Initial research.** Now it's time to verify the short-list. This might take a little longer than shortlisting but by now, you have limited the research to probably about 10 to 20 per cent of the catalogue.

I go straight onto EI Group portal. If you are serious about purchasing in auctions, this portal is a must. More on EI Group in Chapter 5.

Check the postcode on Rightmove and Zoopla – what price would feel like a good price?

Is it possible to do what you intend to do with the property?

Has it been offered in the auction before? When? What was the result? (It takes thirty seconds to check on EI Group.)

3   **Eliminate properties that don't fit your criteria anymore** (i.e. in terms of timeframe, quality of the property, or any other reason).

4   **Focus on the best properties and do full research.** This is where you need to do the serious work that goes into anything that you are investing money in. This kind of research is covered fully in the next chapter.

5   **Optional – Come back to eliminated properties and review again.** After following the process and failing to find something of interest, you might come back with a fresh mind and look at the scrapped opportunities for the second time. Definitely make sure that you address whatever it was that made you eliminate the property in the first place, but keep looking for opportunities.

Do not think of forcing yourself to buy something. However, quite often after reviewing the properties for the second time, you might find things that you have missed out on the first time and suddenly those properties might become a possible deal. Go and do the full research on those newly-discovered properties and ensure they stack up.

CASE STUDY

I once bid on a property for a client in Garratt Lane, Tooting. The property was a house split into two flats without planning permission in place. One of the flats was derelict and the other one was let on an Assured Shorthold Tenancy (AST). The guide price of the property was £550,000+. We knew we could obtain a certificate of lawful use on the property as it had been run as two flats for over four years without any enforcement action and we could find documents to prove that. As two flats in top condition, the block would be worth approximately £1 million to £1.1 million. We were planning to bid up to a maximum of £670,000 but we were outbid and the property sold for £672,000. It was disappointing again but with every bidding comes learning. About two weeks later, I got a notification on Rightmove about an almost identical property, also a house converted into two flats. It was marketed at £695,000 by a local agent. From my experience, agents are not great at marketing complex properties like this. In this case, the property came back to the market as the previous sale fell through. Having had clients prepared with cash, I confidently made an offer of £590,000 with a quick exchange. We finally settled at £630,000 with a delayed completion of three months to suit the vendor's plan and also allow my clients to obtain better finance. So, a lost bidding war allowed us to get a much better deal.

CHAPTER 7

SO, TELL ME WHAT IT'S GOING TO COST & HOW MUCH IS IT WORTH TO ME?

@the.auction.insider In this chapter, I am going to discuss how and why you should be valuing any potential property investments – and as discussed briefly earlier in the book, there will later be a dedicated chapter on exit strategies, which I think will add great value to how you approach a property for investment purposes.

In the first instance, I will go through some of the standard approaches to property valuation, and then I will explain how an auction company takes those valuation approaches and turns them on their head.

@the.auction.pro This is probably the most important chapter of the whole book. You can get all the things right with the other chapters, but if you get this one wrong, you are in deep trouble. Spotting the value and stacking the investment are crucial for any property investors and especially in the auction, you will want to be good and quick at this. This chapter is going to help you with that.

SIMILARITIES AND DIFFERENCES (COMPARABLE EVIDENCE VALUATION)

@the.auction.insider This is the first step taken by many property professionals and more widely by sellers who, before they submit their property for sale, will be looking at what other properties have sold for in the area. What a professional is seeking to do is to look at what has sold and draw as many comparisons to the current property as they can find. Here is a small list of potential varying differences which should be considered after looking at the similarities.

1   Does the property benefit from off-street parking and, if so, what kind of off-street parking? This can vary from a front or rear drive, an allocated underground or overground parking space, all the way through to a separate, attached, or integral garage.

2   Does the property benefit from outside space and, if so, what kind of outside space? This can vary from communal gardens, both front and rear gardens, a patio space, a courtyard, and a balcony all the way through to large grounds and woodland.

3   Proximity. How close is the property to local shops, amenities, transport and schools? It may be that a similar property has sold in close proximity to the one you are valuing, but if it is a quarter of a mile further from local transport links, for instance, this will have a bearing on the valuation.

4 Tax and performance. This relates to taking into consideration the local tax band of the comparable property and the property that you are looking at. A further consideration should be the EPC (Energy Performance Certificate) rating – if the comparable has a 'B' rating and the property you are valuing has a rating of 'E', this should immediately alert you to the possibility that the comparable property potentially had newer windows and doors with a high chance of having newer or better insulation.

All of the above can in various ways contribute to the comparable property selling for the price it did. Now, if the property you are valuing is identical (it is possible), then you can treat the comparable as complete and apply the same end value.

If, however, the property for instance does not benefit from a garage and off-street parking, some may argue that the value is reduced because the property you are valuing does not have the benefit of these additional utilities.

I personally like to look for at least three recent property comparables when I approach the comparable method. It is, however, very rare for me to consider the comparable approach only.

TIME IS MONEY (CAPITAL APPRECIATION ELEMENT)

This is possibly the most subjective part of valuing that I use. It also requires the most amount of work. I have, in previous chapters, spoken about online resources. These resources will have information that can date back anywhere from five to ten years and can highlight how the value of local property changes year on year. What you are looking for here, however, is what the property was worth six, twelve or twenty-four months ago. This will allow you to track how gentle or sharp the capital appreciation for the area is. Remember to look out for results which relate to market, property crashes and recessions. These bits of data are useful when considering base value, but should not interfere with your general valuation.

The HPI (House Price Index) is good for working this out, as is UKLocalArea.com. You may be asking yourself why this specific consideration is important to you. Well, in an upward market, you may look at the speed of capital appreciation and use this as one of your viable exit strategies; for instance, the buy-to-sell method, which entails exchanging on a property, doing almost nothing with it, and allowing a relatively short passage of time to naturally increase its value for you (this normally requires a bullish upward trending market). This can enable you to either complete on the purchase or assign the contract on to another willing purchaser at a higher price.

In the reverse, it will allow you to measure how steep or subtle the incline/decline in the market is, therefore enabling you at the offer stage to build in a (rough) 5–15 per cent equity buffer, which will enable you to ride out most changes in the market, if you allow for time to rectify the market. This is a good approach if you are looking to build a portfolio or indeed, rent and resell within at least eighteen to twenty-four months of ownership (to allow for market correction and the addition of eighteen to twenty-four months of rental income).

NEVER YIELD, BUT ALWAYS BE YIELDING (INCOME PRODUCING CALCULATION)

This is one of the most utilised approaches out there, even in situations when the subject property is currently vacant. It is the landlord/investor's prized calculation.

Rental income (current/estimated/projected) x 52 (if rent is received weekly) or x 12 (if the rent is received monthly), and in commercial property x 4 (if the rent is received quarterly), divided by the purchase price, will equate to the gross yield.

Scenario: The purchase of a property at £120,000 which is let, producing £1,200 per calendar month: the annual income will equate to £14,400.

£14,000 (annual income) ÷ £120,000 (purchase price) = 12% gross yield.

To work out the net yield, I use a simple reverse calculation where I start with the gross income and deduct taxes and expenses to calculate the net yield. I have provided a short list of taxes and expenses below to give you an idea of what to take into consideration:

1   Buying/letting/management fees

2   Landlord/buildings/contents insurance

3   Stamp duty/Income Tax/Capital Gains Tax/Inheritance Tax (personal)/Corporation Tax

4   Professional fees (legal and accounting)

5   Refurbishment costs (wear and tear costs)

There are factors which you can either limit or exclude, such as refurbishment costs and management fees (normally on the condition that you can carry out this work yourself). Remember that in doing so, you will have to calculate an appreciable cost for the rate of your work and time and what the impact of doing this personally may have on your property pipeline. It is certainly viable, if you put together good practices, to keep most of your investments locally to make the above cost-effective and easier to manage.

HOW MUCH DO I GET FOR MY MONEY? (£ PER FT² CALCULATION)

I like to use the £ per square foot calculation when I am looking at an unusual property, or when I am looking at a property with little to no acceptable comparable evidence. I take a cross-section from the local market (ideal would be a good comparable, so a property of a similar size and build) and I take three of the sold prices within the last twelve months.

The next element of the calculation is to look at the size of the property. This can be obtained from several sources.

1 The EPC will contain the m2 (square meterage) of the property.
2 If there is a floor plan, this will normally have the total size in both ft^2 and m^2.
3 If you have access to a site plan (normally available at the Land Registry) which is to scale (this works far better for leasehold properties), you can calculate the internal area of the property.

The calculation to convert the m^2 to ft^2 is to multiply the m^2 by 10.76 in order to ascertain the ft^2.

> **Example: The property measures 60 m^2.**
> **The conversion = 60 m^2 x 10.76 = 645.6 ft^2.**

If, however, you are looking for an easy life, there are a multitude of unit converters online and apps that can be downloaded onto any modern smartphone. Once I have the internal floor area (the habitable space) and the cross section of recent sale prices achieved in the area, I will divide the sales prices by the ft^2. I like to use this calculation on at least three local properties as stipulated above and then use the median of the three to obtain a conservative figure.

YOU GET BACK WHAT YOU PUT IN (RETURN ON INVESTMENT CALCULATION)

The return on investment (more importantly, your capital) is a costing approach that I do not see very often, but it is something that I look at with regards to the investments that I undertake. The principle is simple; the return on investment (the ROI) is a representation of profit after costs. This includes capital appreciation, any added value and income generated.

This process differs from the other calculations insofar as it ties all of the positive uplifts to the property under one calculation (for gross ROI, which can be netted down by deducting costs). Utilising this approach has really enabled me to look at how I profit from a property by giving me the bigger picture, rather than focusing solely on a single element of value within the transaction.

I normally look at the ROI in terms of capital appreciation and added value elements (e.g. planning gain, refurbishment etc.). I normally treat the rental income differently, under a separate calculation. This approach is normally a projection of hope value and therefore, for me, is one of the least viable valuing options I use. I like to investigate this option, as it helps me to assess my exit strategies by forecasting the margins.

In very simple terms, I look at property investments in relation to current value (purchase price), the cost of added value and the potential value. This is all very dependent on the purpose of the purchase and what I am looking to achieve from it.

Obtaining good quality comparable evidence for me is an absolute must. This means not just relying on data available online, it also means making direct contact with local estate agents. This is a step in my valuing routine that I never skip, because it adds so much value and insight from the outset and can normally save me several hours of potentially wasted due diligence.

When looking at yielding property, I always try and consider how well let the property actually is. That means looking at the current rent with scrutiny and deciding whether it is under let, or if I can add value to the property to increase its rentability.

Likewise, I will conduct a cost analysis based on the purchase price (to see where it sits in the local market), and if I am buying in at a below market rate (or below market value [BMV]), I will consider the cost of adding value versus the ease of yielding the asset straight away. When I am looking at trickier purchases, I like to consider the break-up value of the property, which briefly involves splitting the property up into separate pieces and selling those individual pieces off.

For example: a freehold unbroken mid-terrace commercial and residential investment (one of my favourites). I will normally retain the freehold with the commercial property to retain re-sale value and separate the residential units and sell them off as long leasehold flats. The second element should (if done correctly) reimburse you the cost of the purchase, with the commercial unit and freehold retained at zero cost.

START WITH THE END IN MIND: VALUE

@the.auction.pro You should start by asking yourself what value could be added to the property. Can you do a refurbishment? Add a loft conversion? A rear extension? A double-storey rear extension? Excavate a basement? Build another dwelling in the garden? Convert the house into a few flats? Extend the lease on the existing flat? Solve a legal problem with the property to make it mortgageable? Increase rental income? Wait until the end of a life tenancy?

These are only a few ways of adding value. The person who typically ends up winning the bidding is the one who sees the biggest value add in the investment. Even in the case of properties which tend to sell for crazy amounts of money, people tend to see some value that is hidden from others.

CASE STUDY

Two properties in Devon were offered right next to each other. One was an end-of-terrace Victorian house (guide price £200,000) and the other was the neighbouring plot of land of identical size, but without planning permission for a house (guide price £20,000).

The house was quite popular and it sold for £298,000, which was a good result. The plot of land was the most popular lot in the auction with around 100 people registered to bid, including sixteen telephone bidders. Because of the interest, the auctioneer started the bidding at £80,000 and this instantly filtered out half of the bidders. But the bidding did not stop, and it went all the way up to £200,000! For a plot of land where you would need to spend about £150,000 to build a house, worth around £300,000! And that is after you get the planning permission, which was not guaranteed. After the auction, it turned out that the buyers were the same couple who had purchased the house. Their reason for purchasing was that they already lived nearby and all their children wanted to stay on the same street as they did. So, it was not a massive price to pay to have their children live right next door to them. Everyone has their own value in their head and the winning bidder is the one who sees the highest value in the lot!

Important considerations include knowing who your market is and who this property could be most valuable to when finished. This will determine factors such as how much you should expect to spend. If you are looking to refurbish the property and have it let to tenants, then the specification is probably going to be much lower and cost less than if you are going to re-sell the property to an end-user who is likely going to spend a significant portion of their life in the property and will have different priorities to the tenant.

Your target market would also be impacting on the end value the property might achieve. End-users who tend to make more emotional choices than investors are likely to pay a premium for a well-designed space. Investors would also have different cost considerations, such as stamp duty and taxes. The investor would have to pay an extra 3 per cent stamp duty on top of the standard stamp duty. But at the moment, end-users have all sort of incentives. For example, they might even not pay any stamp duty if the purchase is below a certain amount.

The Help to Buy scheme is also known to help developers sell properties at premium prices due to the fact that it makes properties much more affordable to first-time buyers. They might only have a deposit of 5 per cent and that makes it easier to take the first step on the ladder. The price would then be less of a consideration since the government might be lending them the remaining 5 to 15 per cent of the required deposit. In order for your development to qualify for the Help to Buy scheme, you would need to have a minimum of six dwellings, and they need to be within a price range set by the government (currently up to £750,000).

All those considerations will have some impact on the end value of the property. In order to get comfortable with the end values, you need to research the current properties on the market and recent sold prices of similar properties.

Recent sold prices are the most important since they give evidence of actual transactions. Current properties on the market only reflect the asking prices —the prices that investors dream of achieving but which might not necessarily be achieved.

To research sold prices, go to Rightmove sold prices and Zoopla sold prices. Those two sources get their information from Land Registry data and they sometimes include historical information on properties sold that will give you an idea of what you are comparing with. Some historical information that is present on Rightmove might not be present on Zoopla (and vice versa), so it's wise to check both portals.

THE MIDDLE BIT THAT MAKES OR BREAKS THE DEAL

This relates to costs when purchasing and adding value to properties. When purchasing the property, there is a whole variety of costs that are typically overlooked by amateur investors. All they see is the purchase price, refurb costs and end value. In order to ensure that your property purchase stacks up, you need to consider the following costs in your research.

AUCTION COSTS

Each property offered in the auction is unique and might have individual costs attached to it by way of special conditions. Never calculate the bid on your property without seeing the special conditions. They will contain information about extra costs that you as a buyer might be required to pay. They might also contain clauses that require you to complete in a particularly short period of time, e.g. ten days, meaning that you might have to incur higher legal costs and higher finance costs in order to meet the conditions imposed on you. Make sure you include that in your calculations.

The typical auction costs include:

- Auction administration costs (around £750–£1,000 +VAT)
- Buyer's premium
- Reimbursing the seller for the cost of searches (£250–£500 typically)
- Reimbursing the seller for part or all of the selling costs

(it could be anything from 1 to 2 per cent +VAT in most of the sales, but it's not unusual for this to come to even 5 per cent of the costs! It could also be a fixed number such as £5,000 +VAT)

- Reimbursing the seller for their legal costs (£750–£1,500)
- A penalty for missing the completion date (anything from £100 to £500)

Not all of those costs will be applicable to your property, but you need to check each time you are purchasing something.

TRANSACTION COSTS

The costs that are typically overlooked when purchasing the property are the legal and transaction costs.

You will have to employ the solicitor who will charge you for reviewing the legal pack initially and doing the conveyancing after you have won the bid.

The amount your solicitor will charge you might depend on the type of finance you are using and the timelines that you are required to meet. If you are using cash, you are likely to save a few hundred pounds compared with using bridging finance or a mortgage. This is due to the fact that the solicitor will have to communicate more in those instances with the lender's solicitors.

There will also be disbursement such as Land Registry fees to register your title, possibly some indemnity insurance costs, etc. I would add another £250 to cover those.

Other costs to add would be arranging the finance. This might be quite expensive, and we talk about it in the next chapter. You will be expected to pay an arrangement fee of approximately 2 per cent of the loan amount, lender's legal fees of anything between £750 and £2,000 and possibly your broker fee. You will probably also pay for the survey which could cost between £400 and £1,000+ depending on the size and value of the property.

Stamp duty is a very large cost that definitely should be factored in. The stamp duty is a rather complex tax and there are a lot of factors that will affect the amount you will have to pay. Within all our spreadsheets, I have included a Stamp Duty Formula Guide that will allow you to get a guide on the stamp duty you will be required to pay by answering some questions and entering the price of the property. However, you should consult a specialist Stamp Duty accountant who will be best able to advise you (under their indemnity insurance cover) on all the allowances and relief that might be available to you.

EXAMPLES OF COSTS THAT YOU MIGHT INCUR WHILE ADDING VALUE:

1 Refurbishment.
2 Splitting services.
3 Extensions.
4 Lease extension.
5 Tenant eviction.
6 Commercial tenant eviction.
7 Adding floors.

THE MAXIMUM BID

There is a very simple way of coming up with your
maximum bid:
> END VALUE
> *less* COSTS
> *less* PROFIT REQUIRED
> *equals* YOUR MAXIMUM BID

The trick is to have reliable and quality information on all the
ingredients of your maximum bid. One of the ways you can
ensure the quality of information is by involving your whole
team and sharing your observations with them. You can
also approach people who are experienced with this type of
investment and ask them to verify your figures.

WORST CASE SCENARIO BIDDING

Auctions are known for listing properties that might
sometimes be a little risky and uncertain. This might be due
to lack of certain legal documents, inability of the vendor to
produce tenancy documents, lack of planning permission, or
a whole host of other problems. With the short timelines that
are imposed on auction transactions, there might be no way of
getting full information on the particular matter.

In such cases, I always try to get as much information
as possible that would lead to better understanding of the
problems, e.g. if there is a property in the auction offered with

a tenancy on terms unknown and no tenancy documents are being produced, I would try to gather the information from the tenant themselves. You would be surprised what a bottle of wine or a six-pack of beer could do for people's willingness to share crucial information with you that is harmless for them, but could be very beneficial to you.

TOP 5 TIPS

@the.auction.insider We asked Manish Kataria to provide the top five tips for this chapter. Manish Kataria CFA is a professional investor with eighteen years' experience in fund management and UK property investment. He has managed investment portfolios for JP Morgan and other blue-chip investment houses. Within property, he invests in and owns a range of assets including developments, HMOs, BTLs and serviced accommodation. His website InvestLikeAPro.co.uk was set up so anyone can invest like a pro.

In any auction a key variable is, of course, the price which results from the winning bid. It is an important factor but the 'right' price is subjective and varies from one buyer to the next. This is because the same property might be viewed differently by various types of buyers. Using investment terminology, various different strategies can be deployed for the same property. Before buying, be crystal clear about the strategy you intend to employ for that particular property. In turn, that will help determine the right value for you, for that property. Some top tips below:

1 For a **buy-to-sell flip**, know your target buyer market. If targeting investors, they will require a good rental yield. Owner-occupiers, on the other hand, might pay a premium price for a quality finished product. Knowing your target market will determine your maximum entry price.

2 For a **buy-to-sell flip**, be clear on all costs, not just the headline price paid. Other transaction costs include taxes, seller's fees, legal fees, refurb costs etc. These will impact your calculated ceiling price at entry.

3 Again for a **buy-to-sell flip**, be focused on a quick sale. This helps you recycle your capital faster. A quick sale is more likely to be achieved in a liquid/central location.

4 When considering a property for a **buy-to-let**, be clear on tenant demand as well as likely rental values. High rental values, guided by a bullish estate agent, could be a trap if your vacant periods end up being high. A headline gross yield of 12 per cent is only 6 per cent if occupancy levels are at 50 per cent.

5 Strategies such as HMOs or serviced accommodation can fetch higher yields and therefore command a higher purchase price. In this situation, buyers should conduct thorough research into future tenant demand and occupancy. A higher yield can be worth paying a premium for, but only if it is sustainable.

CHAPTER 8
LOOKS CAN BE DECEIVING, SO BE SURE TO LOOK TWICE

@the.auction.insider In this chapter, I'll be going into greater detail on how to get the most value out of viewing the property prior to the auction. I want to pay more attention to this element because, at auction, there is no guarantee of access between the exchange of contracts and the completion. This makes viewing the property and preparing for the auction all the more important.

I have discussed viewing the property in a previous chapter, in relation to free property experience, which looked at viewing a property in terms of what you should bring with you (practically) and really useful information on attending multiple viewings of the same property.

In this chapter, we will discuss how to get the most out of a viewing, what kind of questions to ask and more importantly, what to look out for.

The first step for me is making sure that I do not miss out on any viewing opportunities, so you need to make sure that you register for the property with the auctioneers. Most auctioneers will promote their viewing times on their website and on the property portals. Additionally, some auctioneers will market their viewing times in their auction catalogue. However, I do not like relying solely on the viewing times within the catalogue. Some viewings may be cancelled and/or additional viewings may be arranged, and I do not want to miss out on any additional viewing opportunities. Likewise, I would not want to waste my time on a viewing that may have been cancelled without my knowing.

As discussed in the earlier chapter on viewings, I recommend trying to attend all of the viewings that are practically possible for you to attend. This allows you to measure the level of interest in the property whilst allowing you the opportunity to attend the viewings with your builder/architect in advance.

These viewings present you with every opportunity necessary to make a practical and informed decision. Below is a list of questions to ask, to ensure that you are getting the most out of the situation.

All viewings are going to be conducted by one of the following parties, so your approach and questions will vary, to make sure you have what you need in order to proceed to the auction.

ASSISTED VIEWING: AUCTION PROFESSIONAL

Depending on location and the size of the catalogue, most viewings will be attended by the valuer/surveyor/consultant handling the sale of the property via auction. The following is a short list of good fact-finding questions that will distinguish you from the other viewers.

1 Ask them about the seller – what you are looking for here is to create a basic profile of the seller and to try and understand their selling motivations. Typical questions can include:

   i   Is the seller a property professional?

   ii   Is it a company selling?

   iii Is this a forced sale or a probate sale?

   iv   What is the seller looking to achieve from this sale (this doesn't have to be price)?

2 Is the seller able to consider pre-auction offers?

3 Ask them about the property – this is not an opportunity for them to sell the property to you, but for you to understand their rationale (with regards to the guide price) and where they see the property's end value.

   i   Ask them what they think the property is worth once the value has been realised (this can be once a legal issue has been fixed, a lease extended, a refurbishment completed, etc.).

   ii   Ask them if they know of any structural or legal issues affecting the property.

   iii Ask them what the interest has been like so far.

4 Ask them about the local area and the market – this is a good line of questioning, because it will highlight their experience of recent sales in the area and will give you an insight into how they perceive the market:

   i   Have they sold anything else in the area recently?

   ii   Do they have anything else in the local area for auction?

   iii How was the last auction?

   iv   What do they think about this area?

LOCAL AGENT/DOOR-OPENING SERVICE

If you are gaining access to the property via a local agent, then I would recommend asking the following generic questions, to get the most out of their local knowledge and experience:

1   Ask them what sales are like in the area.
2   What kind of appetite do their buyers have?
3   What is the rental market like locally?
4   What do they think of the property?

ACCESS VIA THE TENANT

If the access is being arranged via the tenant, then this is a great opportunity to interact with them, especially if they will still be renting the property after completion. It may very well be that this tenant will be your tenant, so this is a good chance to gauge their position.

1   For how long have they rented the property?
2   Are they happy there?
3   Is there anything wrong with the property (leaky taps, squeaky doors etc.)?
4   Would they be happy to stay on and continue to rent the property?

ACCESS VIA THE SELLER

This is the holy grail of accessing the property. This is the chance to interact with the person who knows more about the property than the auctioneers and the solicitors put together. This is a great opportunity, but it requires a measured approach. You do not want to appear overly keen, as this may raise their expectations for a sale on the day of the auction.

I would ask the following questions to measure their response and help you to decide on how to proceed. Bear in mind the majority of properties whereby the seller is conducting the viewings are normally owner/occupier sellers and therefore are normally more open to discussion at the viewing.

1   Why are they selling the property?
2   What do they like most about this property?
3   What do they like about the local area?
4   Why did they choose the auction to sell?

It is an important part of the viewing process to reach out and engage with the person enabling access. It is possible that the person enabling the access is a member of a door-opening service; in this instance you are not going to get any real value out of them. The only value here is if you attend the second or third viewing, when you can ask them how many people have attended previously. They are normally quite open on the subject.

BRING A BUDDY

As discussed briefly in a previous chapter, I touched on the idea of bringing someone along to view the property with you. I will be discussing this in far greater detail here. It is important not to waste your time, nor incur any unnecessary costs. With that in mind, do not pay for professionals to attend the property if their knowledge and experience are not required. This is all dependent on your exit strategy and you should keep that in mind before inviting the world and their mothers to attend a viewing with you.

VIEWING #1

For the first viewing, I recommend seeing the property alone. This will enable you to make your own conclusions about the property which are unfettered by other people's opinions or prejudices.

VIEWING #2

For the second viewing, I would recommend bringing a friend or family member along. If they have property knowledge, great, but if they don't, that is fine as well. What you are looking for here is someone impartial, whose vision of the property is not rose tinted.

VIEWING #3

Now it's time for the professional to attend with you, or, far more preferable, without you there. This removes the potential for either party to get carried away and maintains a degree of objectivity.

VIEWING #4

Now that you have viewed the property and have had the benefit of a lay person's impression and the benefit of a professional's observations, you can re-visit the property and really factor in the comments of all those parties, whilst allowing yourself to confirm your initial thoughts.

The type of professional you bring with you really has to resonate with you and agree with your end goal/exit strategy. It is important to think about this, because planning and acting with purpose will save you plenty of time, aggravation and potential cost.

LOCAL AGENT

If you are a regular investor in the local area, and you prefer to buy, refurbish and rent/re-sell, I normally recommend that you invite your preferred local agent. They will value the property as is and may also provide you with an estimated value once the works are completed, although this is just a projection or speculation, and in real terms not worth a great deal. I normally specify that they make their calculations based on a quick sale. This means that they are taking their market into consideration more than just trying to curry your favour.

SURVEYOR

I normally recommend instructing a surveyor, although there are some instances where I think it is a waste of time to do this in advance of the auction. If the property you are looking at is unmortgageable, and you'll have to do works to make it mortgageable, then wait till after the works are completed before you instruct a surveyor. If, however, the property is mortgageable, and you are looking to leverage the property with finance, then getting the surveyor into the property prior to the exchange of contracts is valuable and highly recommended. Additionally, if you have taken a builder to the property and they highlight some issues (structural damage, damp etc.), then I would follow up with a surveyor.

BUILDER/HANDYMAN

For a property requiring either a full programme of refurbishment or just a light refurbishment, I would recommend getting your builder/handyman to attend to provide an idea of cost for the works required. They normally have better sight when pointing out potential defects or issues, and cost those in to their works, potentially removing the risk of unwelcome surprises. This will also help you to effectively gauge your bid price at auction.

PLANNING CONSULTANT/ARCHITECT

With opportunities that include potential for development/ redevelopment/reconfiguration/change of use, then I would recommend making sure that the appropriate party for each of these outcomes attends the property to advise you further. This is especially important due to the frequent changes in local and national planning policy as well as local property licencing. If your exit strategy is a change of use from a single dwelling to provide for either an HMO or serviced accommodation, then additional steps may be required in advance of the viewing, with both the architect and the planning consultant.

PAY ATTENTION TO THE DETAILS

My checklist of things to look out for is non-exhaustive because I find myself looking for different things depending on the property, and depending on what I want to do with the property. I have provided a basic list below for you to use and add to as your knowledge and experience grows. I am basing the below on a mid-terrace house, to help make this list relatable.

EXTERNAL CONDITION

1 **Surroundings** – my focus here will be looking to see if there is any cracking in the pavement outside of the property or in the front garden/yard. I will be looking at the proximity of trees, as well as bus stops. If the property has a garden wall, I will be looking at how structurally sound it is and the

point where the wall and the house meet. I will be looking at the gardens as well, to see how mature the plants and trees are and of course keeping an eagle eye out for Japanese Knotweed.

2   **Brickwork/cladding/guttering** – this is my chance to have a look at the general external condition of the property, especially pointing. Looking at the brickwork and the guttering can give away many clues as to what you might find inside. It will also tell you how well maintained the outside of the building is.

3   **Windows and doors** – I like to make a mental note of the condition and age of the doors and windows, before I inspect them closely. I am normally looking to see if there is any damage around windows or doors (especially on brickwork) and if there is any gapping around the windows.

4   **Roof tiles (front and rear) and the chimney** – I normally take quite a few steps back to get a good view of the roof tiles. Generally, what I'm looking for here is uniformity; that there are no cracks in the tiles and that there are no tiles missing.

INTERNAL CONDITION

1   **Flooring** – normally I am looking purely for aesthetics, but I try and pay attention to the quality and age of the flooring. I like to give the floors a bit of a stamping, especially on the upper floors and in the corners of some rooms (bathrooms and shower rooms), as this can show up structural issues if there has been any flooding or dampness in the past.

2   **Walls** – if you run your hand along some of the walls, you can normally pick up any cracks that have been recently patched. You can also pick up on some dampness, especially in the corners of the rooms. I'm a little old-school so I still like knocking on some walls, especially if my plan is to reconfigure the property. I like to have an idea of which walls are structural and which walls can be moved or removed entirely.

3   **Ceilings** – on the ground floor level, I will be looking for structural cracking and in those rooms that are below any bathrooms or shower rooms, I double check for signs of water damage.

4   **Kitchen** – I look at the general condition of the existing units to see what can be salvaged or repurposed. With regards to the utilities, I pay close attention to the cooker (connections to gas) as well as the sink (and connections to the mains). I will normally take measurements of the kitchen at the same time.

5   **Bathroom/shower room/en-suite** – always be on the lookout for any water damage (mould, cracking, bubbling etc.) and assess if it will need to be replaced entirely, or just in part. I do prefer there to be a window in the bathroom but will settle on a good extractor fan on the condition that the fan is fit for purpose.

It is important to look out for the little things, for instance, some 1950–1970 build properties (area dependent) could have been built with asbestos. This is normally found either in the kitchen or the roof, but asbestos is not limited to those areas. I will be looking for signs of non-standard construction (concrete or timber frame). I am normally looking for these things to cross them off my list, rather than hoping they are there. If they are there, that isn't necessarily a bad thing, but I will alter my approach and my offer.

TOP 5 TIPS

By **Kamil Frost**, an Established Builder (Contractor) and Party Wall Specialist at Frostons Surveyors.
www.frostons.co.uk and www.frostons-surveyors.co.uk

1   **Personal Recommendation** – to avoid disappointment and to build confidence in the development/refurbishment project going forward, relying on a recommendation from a trusted person really makes a difference to your development mindset. Even with the recommendation, always check references and ask for further referrals – it's important to make direct contact and follow up.

2   **Communication** – vitally important prior to purchase to bring your contractor/consultant/architect to viewings and share your projections and plans with them. This approach is based almost entirely on relationships and the formation of a power team. Post completion, the communication will be equally as important to ensure the smooth running of the project and highlighting or mitigating any in-life changes to the development.

3   **Schedule of Works & Contract** – the Schedule of Works may be prepared as part of the production information alongside drawings, specifications, bills of quantities and preliminaries and are likely to form part of the tender documentation and then contract documents. Both client and contractor should engross the contract by witnessed signatures prior to commencement of work. In practice the administrative effort of collating all necessary paperwork can be overtaken by the desire to begin construction. In such circumstances it becomes harder to sort out any disputes relating to the content.

4   **Insurances** – all firms who employ staff are legally required to hold Employers' Liability insurance (EL). EL insurance will help pay compensation if an employee is injured or becomes ill onsite. Public liability insurance is generally required of contractors to provide cover against personal injury or death, or loss or damage to property of third parties such as members of the public or independent sub-contractors. Professional indemnity insurance is there to cover proven negligence on the part of the service provider. The consequences of such negligence on substantial construction projects can be enormously expensive to correct and this type of insurance should, if arranged at the commensurate level, cover your risks. Contract Works Insurance is a policy that covers all risks associated with a construction project, commonly issued under the joint names of a contractor and a principal client.

5   **Party Wall Agreements [PWA] (and Neighbours)** – normally considered between the detailed design (tendering stage of the project) and the application for all relevant permissions. This application requires advance knowledge and negotiation to be navigated successfully. Always consult a professional in these matters. Failure to obtain the relevant PWAs can put a stop on a project even if all other elements have been agreed. It is therefore so important to secure a positive and encouraging relationship with the neighbouring property owners (Freehold and Leasehold). The importance of a Photographic Schedule of Condition Report to evidence and avoid future false claims from neighbours is an exercise of best practice.

BONUS CONTENT

Standard Forms of Contract (Construction):

1   JCT (The Joint Contracts Tribunal)
2   ACA (Association of Consultant Architects)
3   Chartered Institute of Building
4   NEC (The New Engineering Contract): Engineering and Construction Contract)

CHAPTER 9
UNDERSTANDING THE SALE & THE PROPERTY – LEGALLY SPEAKING

@the.auction.insider The legal pack is undoubtedly one of the most important parts of the auction process. For me as an auction professional, I cannot offer a property for sale without a legal pack. For the seller, they cannot sell the property without a legal pack and, likewise for the purchasers, they cannot make an informed decision unless they have the legal pack.

The contents and the timing of the legal pack are of vital importance and both elements have a significant and measurable impact on the sale and success of the property at auction. There are many other factors to consider and I will be addressing those as well.

@the.auction.pro The purpose of this chapter is to provide you with an express layman's training for reviewing the legal packs. I am not going to try replacing your solicitor, but it is important for you to have a basic understanding of the contents of the legal pack in order to ask the right questions, assess the property's value, spot potential problems and get yourself ready for the viewing, or confirm the facts from the viewing day. Your solicitor will still have to review the legal packs on properties that you are looking to purchase, but with the help of this chapter, you will be able to filter out issues before even going to your solicitor, which leaves you able to focus on the auction lots worth pursuing.

CONTENTS EQUAL CONFIDENCE

@the.auction.insider This is where the intentions of the seller and the buyer are closely shared. The seller is looking to offer the property for sale and to have the property sell at a good value. In order for this to happen, the seller needs to supply enough information in advance of the auction to give the buyer the confidence required to bid for the property under auction terms and conditions.

This means that the contents of the legal pack are of the utmost importance. It also means that the legal pack provides the highest level of added value to the property during the auction process.

I have gone through more than a thousand legal packs and I have drafted the following checklists: one based on the minimum required to sell a property at auction; a minimum value-added legal pack; and a belt and braces legal pack. I believe that there should be a best practice legal pack when offering a property for sale, and I think that the best practice legal pack will provide the most value and confidence to a potential buyer and will pay dividends to the seller in return for a potentially higher sales price.

MINIMUM REQUIREMENT LEGAL PACK

1 Land Registry (office copy entries).
2 Energy Performance Certificate (EPC).
3 Tenancy/Lease Agreements (where applicable).
4 Contract (special conditions of sale).

This is the minimum requirement. Although this is a general assertion, there will be one or two exceptions, like commercial property and properties being offered with planning permission.

MINIMUM VALUE-ADDED LEGAL PACK

1 Land Registry (office copy entries).
2 Energy Performance Certificate (EPC).
3 Tenancy/Lease Agreements (where applicable).
4 Contract (special conditions of sale).
5 Local Authority search.
6 Management pack (where applicable).

I call this the minimum value-added legal pack, because there is tangible added-value content, especially in the form of the search pack and the management pack. For me, this is still a basic pack of information, but it shows the buyer that you are really invested in selling the property and that you are willing to add value to the sale with a basic pack of information.

FULL VALUE BEST PRACTICE LEGAL PACK

1   Land Registry (office copy entries).

2   Energy Performance Certificate (EPC).

3   Tenancy/Lease Agreements (where applicable).

4   Contract (special conditions of sale).

5   Full search pack.

6   Management pack (where applicable).

7   Property Information Form (PIF)/Leasehold Information Form (LIF)/Commercial Property Standard Enquiries Form (CPSE) (where applicable).

8   Draft transfer documents (TR1/TR2).

9   Certificates/warranties/indemnities (where applicable).

10 Insurance documents.

This for me is a bit of a catch-all, and all of these documents allow a bidder to attend the auction with confidence, which will be reflected in the sale price. Now, some of these documents may not be applicable, so how do you tell the difference between what is not applicable, compared to what has been deliberately left out?

I recommend a common-sense approach in conjunction with your solicitor. The requirement for this may diminish over time, not as you gain in confidence, but as you gain in knowledge and experience.

There are several sources of information that may not be included within the legal pack, because the information is either publicly available, or easy to obtain by approaching the correct sources (normally local government).

PUBLICLY AVAILABLE INFORMATION

1 **The EPC** – if this is not included within the legal pack, then one of two things may be applicable:

    i   There is no EPC available (especially on properties with Assured, Regulated and Life Tenancies in situ).

    ii The EPC is available publicly on the EPC register.

2 **Planning information** – although I find it handy having all of the planning information within the legal pack, as it saves me time going to the planning portal and downloading the documents separately, I am not put out or upset if I do have to go and forage for it. For me, the planning portal is part of my due diligence, so I would have gone there anyway to see what planning the surrounding properties have.

3 **Local Authority enforcement notices** – these are important notices and they are normally issued following a situation where a development is actioned/completed without planning permission or building regulations.

4 **Tree Preservation Orders (TPO)** – these are important and are always worth noting, especially when your exit strategies include redevelopment or extensions. This can be hampered and outright refused if there are preservation orders over trees within, bordering or within close proximity to the site.

5 **Asset of Community Value Orders** – the existence of an asset of community value order will be picked up in the local authority search, but you will have to investigate this matter further and obtain a copy for your consideration. I

normally see these being registered on public houses and amenities sites (plots of land).

6 **Article 4 areas** – this relates to areas where council-imposed restrictions on conversions are allowed under Permitted Development Rights. There are multiple permitted development rights, and each council has the power to impose restrictions e.g. preventing the conversion of single-family dwellings into houses in multiple occupation (HMOs), amongst other things.

This is a fairly short list. There are, of course, many other sources of information available publicly, but these are the ones that pop up most frequently and can have the most devastating effect if not investigated in advance.

FURTHER INVESTIGATION REQUIRED

I have been thinking about what elements of the legal pack drive me to ask for further information or that may just require clarity before I proceed to either offer before the auction, or ready myself to bid at the auction.

1 Outstanding charges (mortgages or loans)/unilateral notices – I make a point of asking that all charges and unilateral notices be cleared/removed in time for completion. I know that the RICS common auction conditions confirm this, but it never hurts to get it confirmed in writing in advance of the auction.

2   Apportionment of rent clause/reimbursement of rent arrears clause – I know that this one seems obvious, but you'd be surprised how many times this hasn't been picked up and questioned prior to the auction. The apportionment of rent clause for me is unproblematic in residential (rent paid weekly or monthly), because it is easy to calculate the rent payable to the seller between the exchange and completion. For commercial, this can be a little trickier, so I always ask what the apportionment is. With regards to the rent arrears, it is vital that this outstanding amount is factored into your maximum bid price. An additional step for me is to look at how long the tenant has left on their agreement, and if it is close to the end. I will ask them to serve the required notices if I am successful (at my expense); that way I can get a head start on the process and can arrange new tenants. There are very few things in property worse than a void, except having a tenant who isn't paying their rent.

ADDITIONAL COSTS

This is a subject I find myself becoming quite vocal on. The practice of apportioning selling fees onto the buyer is not new, but it has in recent years been taken to the extreme. I remember about seven or eight years ago, it was fairly standard practice for a seller to charge back the cost of the search pack and, if applicable, the cost of the management pack. I found this to be a completely reasonable practice because it is the buyer who takes the benefit of both the search pack and the management pack.

There are now instances whereby the seller is looking to recuperate all costs associated with selling the property, including:

1   Search fees.
2   Management pack fees.
3   Solicitors' fees.
4   Cost of marketing.

These costs are normally highlighted within the Special Conditions of Sale (Auction Contract) within the legal pack. They can be difficult to find, so it is worth paying close attention to the contents of this document, as it is arguably the most important document within the legal pack.

HOW 'SPECIAL' ARE THE SPECIAL CONDITIONS?

As discussed previously, the special conditions of sale, for me, form the main part of the contract of sale. The special conditions of sale detail where the seller/seller's solicitors would like to deviate or amend the RICS' common auction conditions. They will also seek to detail and confirm any non-standard clauses not covered by the RICS. This is normally in relation to a non-standard property offering, or to create more favourable terms.

It is important to note that the special conditions of sale will be stapled to the back of the memorandum of sale and will form the primary terms of the exchange and completion. Sometimes it can be the last document uploaded to the legal pack. There are normally two main reasons for this:

1   The special conditions of sale can either be a pro forma provided by the solicitor to be amended, or they are drafted from scratch. In either event, they will need to be signed off by the seller before they can be uploaded to the legal pack. The requirement for this interaction can and does cause natural delays.

2   In some instances, the special conditions will be uploaded too late, in order to induce buyers to make rash decisions since they may not have had enough time to read, digest and obtain advice on the contents so close to the auction. This naturally precludes people from attending the auction to bid, and in the instances where the property sells, it is normally a disappointing sale, which is represented in the final sales price.

There is no real benefit to submitting the special conditions of sale late. This is a counter-productive approach to the auction process. If you are going to charge fees, that's fine. People will make their own choices, and by submitting the special conditions within good time, it will enable far more people to bid on your property with confidence.

In my opinion, I feel that if fees are to be included within the special conditions of sale, at the very worst, they should be split 50/50, and at the very best, cover the searches and management pack. This approach is more successful in conjunction with the early submission of the special conditions of sale.

RED FLAGS

These are clauses or stipulations that always make me think twice about proceeding. That doesn't mean that I won't proceed; it will just induce me to dig a little deeper before I do.

1. **A non-standard completion time:** Normally a standard completion time is twenty working days (or twenty-eight days if you include the weekends). If the seller is a bank, LPA receiver or a probate sale, then I'd expect the completion time to be anywhere from ten to fourteen days. Likewise, I'd expect small land purchases to have a shorter completion time, due to the lower cost of the land and the relative ease of the transaction.

2. **A non-standard deposit amount:** The standard auction deposit is 10 per cent. This will be the auction house's minimum deposit and will be detailed within the auction catalogue and on the common auction conditions on the website. If the deposit required by the seller is higher, that would raise a red flag and I will do further research into the seller and try to mitigate my risk of over-exposure for the deposit.

3. **Exclusion of the notice period:** The common auction conditions allow for a ten-day notice period if the buyer

fails to complete on time. Some sellers can reduce this down to between five to seven days, and others may remove it entirely. There are plenty of legitimate reasons to do this but I like to find out why, as this is normally linked to their motivation for selling.

@the.auction.pro A typical legal pack would be released about one to two weeks prior to the auction. It would contain the elements described by @the.auction.insider above. I will now describe my approach to reviewing the legal pack for my own purposes, before even approaching my solicitor. This has saved me tens of thousands of pounds in fees on properties that were never going to work for me or my clients, and I had spotted it well before having to engage the solicitor. For those properties that are promising, reviewing the legal pack yourself, even briefly, will allow you to ask better quality questions of your solicitor and make more commercial sense of the purchase.

TITLE DEEDS AND TITLE PLAN

This will show you the extent of the property you are purchasing, and it will also contain all the restrictions and covenants that might be placed on the property. This is really where you should start looking.

Useful questions when reviewing title documents:

1   Does the property extent match what you are expecting to purchase?

2 Are there any restrictive covenants? Would they prevent you from using the property in the way you plan to?

SPECIAL CONDITIONS OF SALE

This is quite a lengthy document and it's standard for all auction sales unless varied by special conditions. Usually it is varied, but it's important to get familiar with it. It deals with all aspects of the sale and sets the conditions in most expected scenarios. If you get familiar with it, you will be able to ask better quality questions of your solicitor in relation to your purchases.

This document, along with the title documents, are the most important parts of the auction sale. It will list all the additional conditions for the sale and those conditions can vary and override all of the standard conditions of sale.

Examples of such variation could be bringing the completion day forward to ten working days instead of the typical twenty working days. It could also shorten the notice period following the missed completion date from the standard ten days to almost any number.

Useful questions to ask when reviewing special conditions:

1 What is the completion date?

2 What are the additional costs on top of the purchase price?

3 Is there anything that really stands out as unusual?

4 What's the minimum deposit amount? Is the deposit larger than 10 per cent of the purchase price?

ENERGY PERFORMANCE CERTIFICATE (EPC)

This will show you the energy efficiency of the property. All properties need to be above F rating in order to be lettable. So, rating might influence how much you might have to spend on the property. The EPC document will also show you the floor size of the property, but be careful on relying on that. It's a good guide but has to be verified as I have seen situations where the floor size on EPC was very different to the real size.

TENANCY INFORMATION

This is essential as it will determine the ways you can use the property until the tenancy is in place and also it will place obligations on you towards the tenant.

It is important to review who the tenancy is with. What rent are they paying? How long is the tenancy? Are they up to date with the rental payments? (This would usually be in the Special Conditions under Tenancy Schedule.)

What type of tenancy is it? Assured Shorthold Tenancy? Regulated Tenancy? Life Tenancy? Assured Tenancy? Common Law Tenancy? Commercial Agreement? Commercial Agreement with protection of Landlord & Tenant Act or outside the Act? License? Tenancy at will?

The type of the tenancy will give you an idea of the kind of responsibilities that will be placed on you and potential ways you will be able to terminate the tenancy and get possession of the property.

With ASTs you also need to ensure that the tenancy was correctly set up and all required documents were served on the tenant at the start of the tenancy (such as Gas Certificate, EPC, How to Rent guide, prescribed information from the Tenancy Deposit Scheme). If not, this will affect your right to serve a section 21 notice to regain possession of the property and could end up costing you a small fortune in legal costs.

The deposit should also be protected in one of the government's regulated deposit schemes in time, i.e. within thirty days of receiving it. If it wasn't, you might be liable for compensation of up to three times the deposit amount, plus return of the deposit. You will also not be able to serve a valid section 21 notice until the deposit has been returned.

With commercial tenancies, this can get very complex and here I would suggest that you let your solicitor educate you on a case by case basis! Another book could be written on this one topic alone.

SEARCHES

Below are the most important searches (i.e. sets of standardised questions and enquiries directed at a local council, water company or some other institution or information holder).

I have also added examples of questions I'd be trying to get answered before handing it all over to my solicitor. Your lenders will be very keen on seeing the searches before lending you the money. Sometimes you can get indemnity insurance to cover you or your lender in a situation where searches are not available. However, this is not an ideal situation and it might expose you to the kind of consequences that might not be covered by indemnity insurance.

LOCAL SEARCH

This is a set of standardised questions and enquiries directed at the local council. They provide various pieces of information they hold on your property and its surroundings that might affect it in one way or another. When reviewing it, I'd be asking these questions:

1 Have there been any recent planning applications? Or any rejected planning permissions?
2 Is the building listed, or is it located in a conservation area?
3 Are there any planning enforcement notices on the property?
4 Are there any planned works that might affect the value of the property (such as new road schemes, train tracks, new buildings etc.)?
5 Are the roads maintained by the council, or are they private?
6 Local land charges – are there any restrictions on the use of the land?

ENVIRONMENTAL SEARCH

This will reveal areas of contamination within a certain radius from the property, i.e. former landfill sites, storage units of dangerous substances, etc. Some of those might affect lending ability.

WATER AND DRAINAGE SEARCH

This will show where the drainage and water pipes are situated. It's quite an important search if you are looking at potential development opportunities with a mains water pipe going through the land, or where a major drain located on the property might prevent development. Study it with caution and ask your planning consultant to review it.

COAL MINING SEARCH

This one would be very important in certain parts of the UK which had former mining activity. This search will identify various mining shafts. This is important from the ground stability perspective. Mine shafts under the property might make insurance difficult to obtain or expensive and they might make lending impossible on the property.

CHANCEL SEARCH

This would reveal any current obligations to pay towards repairing a local church or chapel that affects all property owners in the area. I have not had any problems with this in my transactions, but it's still worth reviewing as liabilities might be potentially high.

THE LEGAL PACK AND ABILITY TO RAISE FINANCE

The contents of the legal pack will have an impact on your ability to raise finance. The lenders require the property title to be free from defects such as restrictions or notices on the property title. They will also be interested in planning permissions, if the property was split into flats or refurbished. They might also require building regulations certificates.

Bridging lenders will be more flexible than traditional mortgage lenders, but you need to bear in mind that in order to come out of a bridging loan, you will need to satisfy the conditions of a traditional lender and for that, you will need a good legal title. So, you need to plan in advance and work with your solicitor, having the end goal in mind.

GETTING YOUR SOLICITOR TO REVIEW THE LEGAL PACK

You might already have a good property solicitor for your property purchases. However, you should find out if they are comfortable with auction transactions. Traditional conveyancing is lengthy, takes anywhere from six to twenty-four weeks and involves getting a mortgage. For an auction purchase this is four weeks or less and requires responding to the bridging lender's solicitor's enquiries immediately. It takes much more for a solicitor to be handling all that effectively, and you should ensure that your solicitor is capable of dealing with all that in four weeks and knows the process your bridging lender requires you to follow. If not, it can end up costing you a lot of stress and money.

When you choose the right solicitor, it is important to communicate to them what your plan is with the property. For example, certain properties might have a restrictive covenant on the title that allows the property to be used as a single-family dwelling only. Using a property against the covenant would be a problem and it can be very easily overlooked by investors. If you are buying a house in order to convert it into an HMO and refinance on an HMO mortgage – then armed with such information, the solicitor can review the legal pack and advise you if there is anything that might prevent you from executing your plan, such as restrictive covenants.

SOLICITOR CHARGES

Solicitors will charge varied amounts for reviewing a legal pack. Reviewing a legal pack places a liability on a solicitor, so they need to charge an amount that is going to be worthwhile for taking on such a liability. Typical charges are between £150 and £400 +VAT depending on the complexity of the legal pack. If you end up purchasing the property, the solicitor would typically deduct this amount from their standard conveyancing charge.

The conveyancing charge will be dependent on how you are financing the property. If it's a straightforward cash purchase, you could expect a better rate. If it's bridging, the cost would be higher since it will require more time to communicate with the lender's solicitor. The amount of time allowed for completion would also have an effect on the price, since it might require the solicitor to drop other things in order to get your transaction handled. Make sure your solicitor is prepared for shorter than usual completion times.

LEGAL PARTNER'S CONTENT

CASE STUDY

***Walking in the Minefield: Case studies of a solicitor's
experience of recent problems in auction sales***

For more than fifty years, Ronald Fletcher Baker LLP has
acted for many sellers and buyers in auction sales. Most are
problem-free but both buyers and sellers can and do face
pitfalls, as can be seen here.

In a recent auction, a commercial property was described
as let on a tenancy at will. The auction pack included a copy
of the tenancy at will in question. The document was headed
Tenancy at Will and contained all the usual clauses one would
expect in a tenancy at will – with one exception. It said that
the landlord could terminate on three months' notice. A
tenancy at will is only valid if there is no provision for notice
and the tenancy can be terminated without notice. This meant
that the tenant had security of tenure under the Landlord and
Tenant Act 1954. After completion, the buyer would have to
give six months' notice to the tenant and then give the tenant
the opportunity of claiming a new lease in court proceedings.
The client wanted to use the property for his own business
and therefore did not bid. The auction seller now might be
facing a claim for misrepresentation from the eventual auction
purchaser, whoever he was.

The same thing happened in a reported case in 2002 when
the auction catalogue described the property as 'being let to
NCP car parks on a monthly licence'. But there was evidence

that the 'licence' was a 1954 Act protected tenancy. What is in reality a tenancy cannot be transformed to a licence by dressing up a 'licence agreement' with certain words. Therefore, the High Court awarded damages to the auction buyer on the grounds of misrepresentation.

Another client had bought a property at auction over ten years ago. The property was subject to two long residential leases. One of the lessees maintained that he had not been given notice of his option to buy the property before the auction sale at the price to be bid by the winning auction purchaser. Having sat on his hands for over ten years, the lessee made a successful claim against our client and forced her to sell the freehold to him at the same price our client had paid over ten years ago (less than half its value). With our help, the client was able to recover all her losses from the solicitor who had acted for her ten years ago and who had failed to ensure that the lessees had been given notice of their pre-emption rights. Any auction purchaser of a freehold property that is subject to existing residential leases must be aware of the tenant's pre-emption rights under the Landlord and Tenant Act 1987.

Another client recently instructed us after successfully bidding for a lease of residential property with only forty-one years left to run. The seller had served the freeholder with a Notice of Claim for an extended lease in accordance with section 42 of the Leasehold Reform Housing and Urban Development Act 1993. This notice proposed a price which the client found very attractive. The notice was assignable to

the auction buyer. After the auction, the freeholder served a
Counter Notice proposing a price more than 50 per cent higher
than the auction seller had proposed. The client was dismayed
to learn that her lenders were not prepared to complete the
advance secured on a lease with so short a term. Luckily, the
Bank of Mum and Dad came to the rescue. After completion
of the auctioned lease, the client completed the purchase of
the lease extension and it turned out the price he paid was far
less than the market value, the freeholder being mistaken as
to what this was. The client could have lost her deposit, but
luckily it all ended happily.

The moral of all this is that there are traps for the unwary
in auctions, and money spent on legal advice before the
hammer goes down is always money well spent.

You can find out more information about Ronald Fletcher
Baker LLP on their website: www.rfblegal.co.uk or by calling
020 7467 5757.

CHAPTER 10
OPPORTUNITIES BEFORE THE BIG DAY

@the.auction.insider I would say that on a daily basis I am asked if it is possible for someone to secure a property prior to the auction. People often try to take this path and usually they are unsuccessful with their approach. I hope that the following will serve as a loose set of guidelines, for you to follow in order to increase your chances of success in the lead-up to the auction.

@the.auction.pro Purchasing before the auction is my favourite way of buying auction properties. It can be very advantageous but it needs to be approached correctly in order to reap benefits. What @the.auction.insider is saying below is extremely useful. Towards the end of the chapter, I expand with my top five tips of being successful at making pre-auction offers.

MANAGING THE SELLER'S EXPECTATIONS

@the.auction.insider Normally when people are making offers, they are looking at what they would like to achieve, and usually forget that there is another party in the equation.

It is important not only to know why the seller has submitted their property to the auction, but to also gain a measure of their expectation. In this regard, it is important to look at the generic types of seller at auction and their driving forces.

1 **The disappointed/frustrated seller:** This is the owner/ occupier portion of the seller demographic. They are normally submitting the property to the auction because they have had the property on the market for a significant amount of time, and one of the following has taken place:

   i   It may be that the seller had received a good amount of interest, which has either progressed to the offer/ exchange phase, but for one reason or another, it has not sold. Normally in this situation, the reason can be as simple as a collapse in the chain.

   ii It may be that the seller has had the property on the market and has not received any proceedable offers or interest. This can be a result of unrealistic expectation, desperation on behalf of the agent to just win the business at any cost and keep their window displays full, or there may be a real issue affecting the property, which makes the property less desirable to the open market.

In this situation the seller has agreed to submit their property to the auction because it has a defined timescale (if sold), it is not subject to a chain and the deposit is non-refundable – providing an additional layer of comfort, especially if they have experienced failed transactions in the open market.

The sellers in both situations will have accepted an auction valuation, which is normally less than the open market price, and would be hoping for an uplift on this lower price with competitive bidding on the day of the auction. An offer from a seller like this will need to be representative of a fair value. They are normally marketing to the emerging owner/occupier buyers at auction. This is a smaller part of the market, but an active part nonetheless.

2 **The nimble trader:** This is the small to medium-sized investor who has normally sourced their properties direct, and their primary exit strategy is to sell their recent purchase via auction. If it doesn't sell, they will normally commence works and then re-sell via a local estate agent. They prefer the auction sale, for the same reasons the disappointed/frustrated seller does. This is a very precise artform; it requires the trader to not only cost in their profit, but also entice their auction buyer to bid. This means that they have to be able to secure a property at a level appropriate enough to factor in the profit margin of at least two sales (their purchase and that of their buyer). There are, broadly speaking, two types of trader at the auction:

i **The assignable contract trader:** In a situation like this, the seller at the auction is selling their contract of exchange and will normally arrange for their completion to take place at the same time as the designated completion for the buyer at the auction. This is also referred to as a 'back-to-back'. There is nothing inherently wrong with this practice, but I would recommend that your solicitor makes the requisite pre-contract enquiries of the seller's solicitor, to ensure that they are in a position to sell and pass title to their client upon completion.

ii **The portfolio trader:** This is the far rarer of the two generic types of auction trader. This is normally a landlord with a large portfolio. They access the auctions to buy and to sell in staggering volumes. The work here is to maintain a continuous flow of properties, which powers their investing machine. They are not always the most pressured/motivated to sell, but have an accurate grasp of the market and the value of their properties. They appreciate opportunity and are always looking to do a deal.

Dealing with a trader pre-auction is normally fairly clean cut; they know what they want and are happy to enter into discussion. There can be some games played if a trader is looking to make an offer on another trader's property. The important thing to remember here is that there is a deal to be done and this type of seller will normally look to secure an underwrite offer prior to the auction.

3 **The added value seller:** This type of seller can technically be classed as a trader, but what makes them different is that they are likely to add some value to the property from their point of purchase to their point of sale. I like to separate the added value sellers into three generic types:

i **Material added value:** The addition of granted planning permission, a new tenant (yielding the property) or completing a light refurbishment. There are many more options, but these are some of the more common examples. Here, the seller has taken a physical action to effectively increase the value of the property.

ii **The added hope value:** Here, the seller has taken a less direct approach to adding value. This can include obtaining positive pre-application advice for a potential development, the serving of legal notices, for instance a section 42 notice (required to increase a short leasehold property), gaining vacant possession from either an Assured Tenant, Regulated Tenant or Life Tenant.

iii **The problem solver:** This seller has normally undertaken some legal work in order to resolve an issue, which otherwise would have made the property either unmortgageable or unsaleable. Situations include resolving enforcement notices, forfeiture of lease applications, boundary issues and adverse possession.

These sellers are normally ready to do a deal, so they can go back to the market and start the next project. Normally, the properties they are taking on are unmortgageable, which means that they have a lot of cash tied up in the sale. A respectable offer is likely to be taken seriously but expect to haggle. They have added value, so cannot be judged entirely on the price they had paid for the asset.

4 **The institutional/corporate seller:** These sellers are normally the hardest type of seller to approach prior to the auction. They are normally bound to some degree or other

with a fiduciary duty to their client. Institutional/corporate sellers include:

i   Banks/building societies

ii   LPA receivers/fixed charge receivers

iii Pension funds/charities/trusts

The seller is normally not emotionally invested in the sale but is using the auction to discharge its requirements to ensure an open and unfettered sale to achieve a fair and reasonable price. This type of seller is normally far more approachable post-auction (which we will discuss later).

5   **The motivated (non-property professional) seller:** You will find that the majority of sellers who fall within this category are acting in advance of one of the institutional/corporate sellers taking control over their asset and selling on their behalf. Another motivated seller is normally someone whose circumstances have changed drastically, and they need to realise the asset's value in a very short time. In this category, I also add the probate seller – they are quite keenly motivated to sell in accordance with terms of the will, and they too will be bound to achieve an open and unfettered sale, which is why the auction method is so attractive to them. The sale has to be quick and certain to incentivise them to sell prior to the auction. This type of seller will normally stay clear of the underwrite option, and will strongly consider a sale prior to the auction, and even more so if you are able to complete earlier than stipulated.

Now you know the generic types of seller and their general motivations, this should help you to narrow down the properties you are looking to bid on pre-auction and moreover, how to approach that seller.

TIMING IS EVERYTHING

I have discussed the importance of timing already and this is something that is vitally important to the success of your offer. There is a sweet spot of submitting offers prior to the auction and for me that is usually between the second/third viewing, and the availability of the legal pack. There is also a metric, which shows that an offer submitted within seventy-two hours before the auction may capitalise on the seller's uncertainty, or 'cold feet'.

I would never recommend submitting an offer before the first viewing and when there is no legal pack available. All this does is highlight to the seller that the property is very desirable and that they could possibly achieve more for the property through competitive bidding in the auction.

When making the offer prior to the auction, it is important to be able to entice the seller out of the room with practical and appreciable incentives:

1   Offer a shorter completion date.
2   Offer the underwrite option.
3   Offer a premium.

There are other ways to secure the property via auction. This normally entails a written offer (all offers have to be in writing) detailing why you are possibly the only realistic purchaser for the property. For instance, a short leasehold house with less than seven years left on the lease. If you are the freeholder, you are the primary option. If you have significant experience with short leasehold houses and are not the freeholder, then you have positioned yourself at the top of the offer pile and are most likely going to be successful due to this inducement.

Timing, and the means in which you relay your offer, are important. This is your handshake with the seller and you setting your stall out for business. It has to be a clear, concise and actionable offer. This sometimes will be the element that people pay the most attention to when deciding which offer to go with.

Remember to consider the seller's position when making pre-auction offers and consider your timing of the offer to manage the seller's expectations. There is a bonus chapter detailing the underwriting option below. I now put forward an underwrite offer on all of my offers as well as a buy-it-now price. The approach of the offer doesn't change much at all, only the outcome.

It is important to submit your offer professionally and to state how you got to your offer if you are submitting an offer under or at the guide price. This will make a big difference in the acceptability of your offer. Finally, make sure that you are in a position to follow through with your offer: an accepted offer prior to the auction has the same gravitas as the fall of the hammer at auction. It is a legal exchange of contracts.

FIVE STEPS FOR SUCCESS WITH PRE-AUCTION OFFERS

@the.auction.pro

1 Discreetly find out who the vendor is. In order to do that, some of the following steps can be useful:

    a Check auction entry for information saying 'By order of' e.g.

        i Executors

        ii LLP receivers

        iii Mortgagee

        iv A major fund etc.

        v Local Borough Council

        vi Housing Association

    b Check the legal pack:

        i Land registry entry – quite often the names might be redacted but this would only stop an amateur. As a pro, you know you can download your own title document from the Land Registry by paying £3.

        ii Check replies to enquiries (if available) – those documents will have the name of the person completing the documents (normally the ' seller) – very rarely would the seller's details be redacted there.

        iii Check planning permission (if available) – quite often the applicant name might be the owner or his agent.

        iv Google the address of the property with the full postcode and see what comes up.

2   After all that, call the auction house and ask some questions. Don't pretend you know everything about the property; be humble, even if you know a lot. It helps to learn more information. Don't be fazed by some dismissive responses from the person on the phone – this might be yet another call of many about that particular property. Be persistent and ask inquisitive questions.

3   Don't be too impatient when making pre-auction offers. Offers made within the last seventy-two hours before the auction tend to be the most successful. When making an offer, make sure you position yourself as a capable buyer. The first person you need to convince of your abilities is the auctioneer. Say you are aware of whatever issues the property might be affected by, say you have done your research and reviewed the legal pack, say your finds are in place and you are ready to exchange immediately. This is the way of ensuring that your offer is taken seriously and sounds good to anyone.

4   Your pre-auction offer needs to speak to the vendor's motivations. Would they be motivated by faster completion? Guarantee of the sale with possible upside (underwrite) or premium price?

5   If your offer is rejected, do not worry – you might get it cheaper in the auction or even post-auction.

CASE STUDY

I came across a one-bed flat in Thornton Heath that failed to sell in the auction. Having had a brief chat with the vendor, who was at the auction and disappointed with the lack of sale, I had tried to establish the price the property could be purchased for. The reserve disclosed after the auction was £155,000. We were not willing to go that high. The property was re-entered into the auction at a guide price of £120,000. This time we were determined to get it pre-auction at a price of £140,000. Our offer was rejected! The vendor wanted a minimum of £150,000. So, we waited and we went to the auction. It turned out we were the only bidders and we got the flat for £130,000, £10,000 less than we were prepared to offer prior to the auction. My client was extremely pleased. The moral of the story is that pre-auction can be good, but a rejected offer doesn't mean a lost deal!

INSURING YOUR PURCHASES

@the.auction.pro Insurance is often a forgotten part of the transaction. Most of the properties at auctions are purchased at the buyer's risk from the moment of exchange of contracts. When you exchange contracts, you are committing to complete on the transactions sometime in the future (normally four weeks from the auction). There are a lot of things that can happen between exchange and completion (fire, flood, malicious damage etc.) and you will still be obligated to complete, no matter the condition of the property. This is such an important part of the transaction that we have asked our preferred insurance partner, Insurance Desk, to provide content and their contact details within this book. If you are in a rush to get insurance and all the buzz of the auction is present, it's easy to miss important aspects of the cover or overpay for what you need just to get the cover. Some properties might be especially challenging to insure, as a lot of insurers have various exclusions. Insurance Desk provides us with insurance advice, hence we have no hesitation recommending them within our book.

INSURANCE DESK – PARTNER'S CONTENT

www.insurance-desk.com

01296 329610 Josh Munt Head of New Business

www.insurance-desk.com/auctions

The outcome of an auction is always uncertain, but if you secure the property you want, you need to move quickly and Insurance-Desk.com is here to help you cover your new acquisition on the same day by offering advice and recommendations.

As your property insurance broker, we can provide advice and quotes for specialist insurance contracts covering long-term empty buildings, properties undergoing minor and major works, houses with sitting tenants, mixed-use commercial, offices, shops and warehouses – pretty much any property type.

It is vital to make sure you protect the building and, ultimately, yourself. We have seen individuals who have incurred huge financial loss having not done the basics and sought the correct advice.

DON'T AVOID RISK – MANAGE IT!

You've just bought the property you wanted and the buzz is still with you. It is times like this when it is all too easy to forget what's important, such as ensuring you have the correct cover in place.

Many properties that appear at auction are vacant and require specialist insurance. Most insurance policies offer fire, lightning, explosion and aircraft cover (FLEA) only. It is vital to get a policy that will include water, storm, malicious damage and theft.

A story we hear all too often is that a property has been broken into and the boiler has been stolen, resulting in severe water damage. Without the proper cover in place, this can be a costly problem to solve.

CASE STUDY

For one landlord it was an experience he will not forget, **resulting in £23,000 worth of damage**. *He thought he had insurance in place, but unless you read your policy in depth it can end up being a financial nightmare!*

The property, which should have been turned over in eight weeks and made a profit, took sixteen weeks, with the cost doubling due to the common mistake of the wrong cover being in place. The property made a loss.

Another landlord/property investor told us of his repudiated claim with an insurance company. This happened because the building was long-term empty and he thought the sixty-days-empty cover began when he purchased the property. We have access to companies who are happy with insuring long-term empty property. In this case, the property was empty for twelve months before the person purchased it at auction, so having the correct cover was key. **This cost him £37,000!**

INSURANCE NEVER PAYS OUT – I'LL CHANCE IT!

We constantly hear from individuals who purchase properties at auctions that they feel it's not worth their while adding insurance as it's just more money being spent. Indeed, these individuals often feel that spending £35,000 renovating a property is an investment and yet, a few hundred pounds spent on insurance is an expense – both should be seen as shrewd investments.

Just think, YOU are responsible for damage caused to individuals who get injured in your empty building, for example, falling roof slates, tiles, brick, etc. The claims for these cases can run into hundreds of thousands of pounds and often more.

This can be the case, for example, even if someone is near your property or grounds illegally – a recent example was a young child swinging on the rusty gate of an empty property. He suffered severe head injuries when the gate gave way and landed on the concrete. It was deemed that the gate should have been either removed from the property or made safe. The property owner was insured and the claim for £1 million was settled by the insurance company.

TOP FIVE TIPS: HELP YOUR BROKER TO HELP YOU

1 Don't leave it to the last minute – trying to arrange cover on a Friday at 5 p.m. is not ideal.
2 Make sure the cover type is correct for what you are planning – if you plan to renovate and then let the property out post-renovation works, you may need two policies to

run consecutively. Alternatively, some specialist landlord policies can cover minor works so you don't have to worry about cancelling one policy and starting another one.

3 If the property has been long-term empty, make sure this is fully disclosed.

4 Give a list of minor/major works you are planning to do.

5 Make sure the property is insured for the correct amount, or the 'reinstatement value'; this is NOT what you purchased the property for, or what you feel it's worth. The reinstatement value is the cost of rebuilding the property again from top to bottom and is often found from a RICS surveyor's notes in any finance or mortgage offer. Failing this, you can work out the figures at https://abi.bcis.co.uk/calculator/.

Insurance-Desk.com has access to a number of insurer markets to ensure that we find the best price and cover and we will be able to provide the cover the same day.

Remember, we will need the following to get a quote:
- Property address
- Construction (brick, tiled roof, flat roof, etc.)
- Rebuild value (not market value)
- Condition of the property (please remember existing damage is not covered)
- Security
- Your plans for the property, i.e. when do you expect it to be occupied?

CHAPTER 11
FUNDING YOUR PURCHASE

@the.auction.pro This chapter is all about your ability to purchase the property you want to bid on. There are a variety of ways to go about arranging finance on auction properties. The one that is most suited for you will depend on the time you have to complete on the transaction, and also on the state of the property that you are purchasing (in both a legal and structural sense!).

CASH

This is the easiest way of purchasing the property. When one is buying the property with cash, you don't have to be bothered with lender's requirements, and you are in a position to move as quickly as required by the transaction. However, there are dangers of buying fully in cash. When your solicitor is acting for you while you are using a lender, they will have to ask all the questions that the lender will want answers to. There is no such requirement when you are purchasing property with cash. Your solicitor might pick up on the most important things, but in order to make sure that you will be able to refinance the property, you should be thinking like a lender, even when purchasing the property with cash. It will save you hassle and disappointment when trying to refinance or sell the property to a buyer who will be taking finance.

The things to especially look out for when buying properties in cash are:

1   Are there any restrictions or enforcements, and what would it take to remove them to satisfy the future lender?

2   Do the physical boundaries of the property match the lease/ title plans?

3   Are there any legal problems with right of way?

4   What is the size of the property? Is it more than 30 m²? (Typically, lenders don't lend on properties smaller than that.)

5   Are there any structural issues? Can they be repaired?

6   Is the type of the property mortgageable or is it a typical cash purchase?

7   Is the EPC above F? How much would it cost to bring it to E or above?

TRANSACTION COSTS

You will need a substantial amount of cash for your auction transaction, no matter what kind of finance you are using. There are costs that the lender will not be taking into consideration and you will need to pay for them directly. I always recommend that, as a rule of thumb, you have at least 40 per cent of the purchase price ready as cash.

The costs include:

1   Stamp duty (for the advance stamp duty formula, go to the resources page of our website).

2   Auction admin fee (about £1,000).

3   Special condition costs (anything from zero to 5 per cent of the purchase price in extreme cases).

4   Survey costs (usually around £500–£1,000).

5   Solicitor costs (around £1,000 to £1,800, but highly dependent on the complexity of the purchase).

6   Refurbishment costs (if applicable), although there might be products that will allow for refurbishment costs to be covered.

7   White goods/furniture for the property after refurbishment (if applicable).

8   Lease extension costs (if applicable).

9   Running costs of the property while it's empty (council tax, utilities, service charges, business rates, etc.).

10 Costs of evicting the tenants.

11 Costs of arrears of existing tenants (if purchasing a tenanted property, you might need to reimburse the seller for the arrears and in return, you get assigned the right to recover those from the tenant).

As you can see, there are a lot of costs that you need to consider and have cash for. Some of them can be paid using credit cards, personal loans, etc. but being aware of those costs well in advance of the auction helps with setting up your maximum bid at the level that will leave you in profit at the end of the project, and without too much financial strain.

BRIDGING FINANCE

Bridging finance has a reputation for being a very expensive and risky type of finance. And it can be. However, it's a very useful way of financing auction transactions if you know what you are doing and are using the bridging finance for what it is intended, i.e. creating a bridge between where you are now, and where you are expecting to be in six, nine or twelve months' time.

Bridging finance is a short-term solution, designed to allow you to transact, with a view to replacing it with long-term finance at the end of the term. This is why you need to have very clearly defined exits to be successful with using bridging finance. In my opinion, it's very easy to get bridging finance. The bridging lender takes quite a low risk compared to the investor. They only lend 70 per cent value of the property and the investor is putting in the 30 per cent deposit. Normally, interests are rolled up and deducted from the loan at the start, meaning that the net loan is somewhere around 60 per cent of the purchase price, leaving the investor with 40 per cent of the deposit required. Bridging finance is typically secure with first charge, meaning the lender can repossess the property and sell it to clear the debt. And for the lender, it will normally be quite easy to clear the balance if all they have to do is sell the property for at least 70 per cent of the value.

WHERE TO GO TO GET BRIDGING FINANCE

The competition in the market of bridging loan providers is very high and there are lots of firms offering this type of lending. It might be tempting to approach bridging lenders directly and get a good deal by bypassing the broker. However, I'd suggest that using a broker goes well beyond just arranging bridging finance. The most important role of the broker is understanding your property and your circumstances in terms of the exit strategy. As mentioned, getting the bridging is easy, but repaying the bridging loan might be trickier, and with that in mind, you will want to have a team that is acting for you in order to set things up efficiently. Any delay in repaying the bridging loan over the agreed period might cost you dearly, so it pays to have a broker.

The broker will also give you access to deals that might not be available directly from lenders. Remember that brokers have relationships with lenders that go beyond just one deal, and that mutual relationship can allow for better terms of the deal when it really matters.

The costs of bridging loans can vary from as low as 0.44 per cent per calendar month (pcm) to as high as 2 or 3 per cent per calendar month. Typical variables that decide the rate are:

1 **Type of property**
   i   Residential is normally less expensive
   ii   Commercial is more difficult to finance
   iii Developments – it all depends on experience

    iv Land with no planning – it's usually quite a risky purchase, hence a bit more expensive

2 **Loan to value**

    i The higher the LTV, the more risk for the lender and higher the interest rate

    ii Highest LTV is normally 75 per cent secured

    iii Typical LTV on commercial properties is about 65 per cent

3 **Speed of transaction**

    i The quicker you require the money, the more you will have to pay, as the lender will be required to take a view on certain aspects of the transaction, making it riskier and hence requiring more money

    ii Lenders know when you are desperate. If money is required quickly, they will be less flexible on their terms as they know you are likely to accept them anyway

    iii Some purchasers find cash to purchase the property and then they proceed to get a bridging loan as they no longer need to draw down the loan very quickly and because of that they are in a better position to negotiate more favourable terms with the lenders.

4 **Length of the loan**

    i Quick loans of three to six months are less expensive than longer loans

    ii For any loan, there is usually a 2 per cent arrangement fee – so with a three-month loan, you might end up paying relatively more in total, even if the interest rate is lower.

COSTS OF ARRANGING BRIDGING FINANCE

The costs of arranging bridging finance will vary from property to property. Depending on all the factors mentioned above, there might be factors that will make the loan more expensive. Your broker should be able to advise you on a case-by-case basis, but the typical costs of arranging bridging finance will include the following:

1 **Broker fee if applicable:** Usually an application fee of around £500 is charged, although most brokers are paid generously by bridging lenders so they might waive this fee

2 **Lender's arrangement fee:** Typically, 2 per cent of the loan amount – normally deducted from the advance

3 **Lender's legal fees:** Normally, about £1,500 +VAT, although it might vary. It's an upfront cost once you accept the initial terms of the loan and proceed to the legal part

4 **Survey costs:** Depending on the type of property, this is normally between £500 and £1,000 for a residential property. It depends largely on timings – sometimes surveyors might charge a premium for quick surveys. Commercial surveys might require more input and hence the commercial surveyors might even charge up to £2,000. It's not unusual for surveys for very expensive apartments to cost £20,000 to £50,000. It is all connected with the risks that the surveyor takes, as that will increase their Professional Indemnity insurance costs and therefore needs to be reflected in the price.

5 **Interest costs:** Most lenders retain six or twelve months' interest at the start of the loan, unless you can prove that the loan can be serviced monthly from either the property income or your personal income.

Some of the costs above can be added to the loan, but that means that the net advance will be reduced by those costs. The gross loan cannot exceed 70 or 75 per cent LTV but, after deductions, you are likely to only receive 55 per cent to 65 per cent of the purchase price as an advance.

As an example, you purchase a £250,000 property in the auction. The bridging company is willing to lend you 75 per cent of the purchase price, i.e. £187,500.

The arrangement fee is 2 per cent of that amount, so £3,750. It gets deducted from the gross loan amount.

The lender's legal fee is £1,800 incl. VAT and this gets deducted from the loan amount.

The loan is at 1 per cent per month for twelve months and all interest amounts are rolled up and deducted up front. If you repay the loan before the twelve months, you will be reimbursed the interest for the unused period. The interest amounts at 1 per cent per month and over the twelve-month period works out to £22,500.

Total deductions work out to £28,050. So, the net amount of the loan you will receive is approximately £159,450 and you will need to pay the balance of the £250,000 out of your own cash. This means you will need to find £90,550 in cash, plus all the transaction costs such as stamp duty, auction costs and refurbishment costs. The cash input required on this transaction is likely to be about 40 to 45 per cent of the purchase price.

EXITING A BRIDGING LOAN

Exiting a bridging loan is the first thing you should be thinking about when taking it out. As mentioned before, a bridging loan is meant to be just that – a bridge. You need to know what the destination is to successfully use the bridge. Otherwise, you will end up in the hole!

The exits that are available for you to repay the bridging loan might consist of:

1   Selling the property after adding value
2   Refinancing the property onto a long-term product
3   Raising funds from another property or source to repay the loan
4   Refinancing onto another bridging loan (risky!)
5   Extending the term of the bridging loan (risky!)

You need to be very clear how you will be adding value to the property and what kind of lending might be available to you (or your buyer) on the exit. If you are thinking of refurbishing and tenanting the property, make sure you work through the scenario with your broker and satisfy yourself that the property and the income produced will satisfy the lender, in order to raise enough funds to repay the bridging loan.

If you are selling the property, ensure you incorporate enough contingency time to allow for one or two months of marketing and an extended conveyancing period.

There are several products available on the market that are so-called bridge-to-let products. They allow you to plan the exact exit from the bridge. Bridge-to-let products are available on properties that require light refurbishment and sometimes even heavy refurbishment. You initially borrow on the bridging terms, but the surveyor will value the property in the current condition and also work out what it would be worth after the works are completed. Once the works are completed, the surveyor needs to verify that all has been done, and then the lender will transfer your lending onto a new product that is designed for long-term lending. At the end of the chapter, one of our expert brokers will explain exactly such a scenario.

100 PER CENT AND ABOVE BRIDGING

There are investors who might not exactly have all the cash in their account, but who are asset-rich. They might have one or many properties sitting around without, or with, very little lending on them. Some lenders would be happy with taking such properties as collateral for the lending and lend you 100 per cent or even more of the purchase price. The rule is that the security on both properties may not normally exceed the lender's maximum LTV – so typically 70 or 75 per cent LTV. This type of lending is rather advanced and you need to plan well, otherwise the costs can accelerate very quickly.

MORTGAGES

Mortgages are not impossible to obtain on auction properties, but they are risky to rely on as your only means to finance your property.

The problem with mortgages is that they can take quite a long time to arrange, as underwriters are used to a normal type of conveyancing when time is not as crucial. In the auction scenario, the time to complete is limited and the lender might not be ready to act as quickly as you require.

Mortgage lenders are also much more thorough than bridging lenders in reviewing the legal pack and the title of the property. They may require documents that are either not available in the legal pack or might take a long time to obtain.

One such document is a local search. Most lenders require an official local search from the council. This may take two to four weeks to obtain. Most auction sellers do provide a local search, but it's normally only a so-called personal search, prepared by a specialist company. In most cases, it's very quick to obtain, it contains the exact same information that official searches do, but lenders still don't like relying on personal searches. This small issue could delay the process of obtaining finance well beyond the four-week completion period and expose you to breach of contract.

That is why the ability to arrange a mortgage should be only a bonus.

In order to increase your chances of arranging a mortgage on the auction property, you need to follow these guidelines:

1. Ensure the property has a functioning kitchen and bathroom and can be classed as habitable.

   i. 'Habitable' can be quite flexible. It does not mean you would want to move in there. It means that if you were forced, you could function in the property and perform basic tasks.

   ii. It's important that the property only has one kitchen if it is a house or a flat. Otherwise, it might be classed as having a risk of being used as multiple dwellings and be struck off as unsuitable for mortgage lending until the second kitchen is removed.

2. Ensure the legal pack is sound. Ask your solicitor before the auction to review the pack with an eye to things that might be of concern to a mortgage lender. A good solicitor will be able to advise you on possible issues, although they might not be able to make guarantees.

3. Ensure the lease on the property has at least eighty years on it. If it's shorter, there might be lenders who will be prepared to lend on leases above forty years, but the choice is very limited.

4. Ensure that the structure of the building is not non-standard.

   i. Non-standard constructions include some types of concrete-frame Wimpey-fines (unmortgageable), Wimpey no-fines (there are limited lenders), steel-frame construction, Cornish-type construction

5. Ensure that the property is not above commercial properties classed as high-risk, such as takeaways and restaurants, car repair garages, etc.

6 Ensure the height and number of storeys is not too high for your lender's requirements. There are a limited number of options in properties above five storeys.

7 Ensure your personal circumstances will allow you to obtain the mortgage. To do this, it's best to obtain a decision in principle, which will essentially class you as a good borrower and will be subject to property due diligence.

CROWDFUNDING

This new way of financing property transactions is on the rise. There are several crowdfunding platforms set up which are raising millions of pounds from the public. For the public, it offers an easy way to invest smaller sums of money into property and earn a good income which is secured on the property (typically!).

For the borrower, the costs of using crowdfunding websites are not too dissimilar to bridging finance. But it allows for two things. One is raising finance and bringing their own investors/family members etc. through a platform that is FCA-regulated. There are now a lot of regulations regarding pooled investments and joint ventures, and some investors prefer bringing their investors to regulated crowdfunding websites in order to meet the compliance requirements.

The second reason lenders raise funds through crowdfunding is to raise their own profile in the process. Crowdfunding can be a very good marketing tool for property developers and their businesses.

COMMERCIAL FINANCE

Commercial finance is suitable for either commercial property (surprise, surprise!) or mixed-use property with commercial and residential elements or blocks of flats that are financed all in one transaction.

Commercial finance will share quite a lot of characteristics with standard mortgages. It might take quite a lot of time to arrange and there will be a lot of questions to ask.

This type of finance is suitable for income-producing properties. It's got almost nothing to do with the bricks-and-mortar value of the property. It's all to do with income, the security of that income and strength of the covenant, duration of the leases or tenancies and the location of the property.

It's normally quite difficult to arrange commercial finance in time before completion of the auction transaction, hence the usual way to do it is to arrange a bridging loan first and then refinance onto a commercial product.

PRIVATE LENDING

This is something that I use quite a lot in my purchases. I like working with friends, family members and people from my circle who have funds sitting around, but no inclination to make their own property investments.

There are strict regulations around pooling together lots of investors and marketing the investments or opportunities. It's a very risky area. If you want to stay safe, only work with people you already know. Do not bring more than one investor into your project. Always do proper loan agreements and take the borrowers' ID and proof of address. You will need to satisfy yourself and your solicitor of the source of the funds and prove where they come from – including where your investor has sourced them.

If you are thinking of pooling investors together, think about using a crowdfunding platform, as they are regulated and will ensure that your funding is fully compliant. It costs about 5 per cent in arrangement fees; however, if you fail to properly handle investors' money, it will cost you much more and can even lead to a spell in prison.

MORTGAGE DESK – PARTNER'S CONTENT ON DEALING WITH FINANCE

@the.auction.pro John Cox, mortgage broker and short-term finance specialist at Mortgage Desk is our preferred finance partner to deal with auction properties. As mentioned in the chapter already, getting bridging finance is extremely easy as long as you have enough of a deposit. However, you should have in your team someone who will also help you exit the bridge and, for us, Mortgage Desk is the preferred place to go.

WHY OPT FOR SHORT-TERM FINANCE?

1 It can be secured against nearly any site with any use including residential, commercial and land
2 Proof of income is not always required

3   Applications can be completed in just one week

4   Deals are bespoke to each application and client to suit their specific needs

5   Benefits of speed

6   Rates from 0.43 per cent pcm

7   Up to 80 per cent LTV and 100 per cent with additional security

8   No maximum loan, with terms from one day to twenty-three months

9   Adverse credit can be considered

CASE STUDY

Commercial Unit Development Opportunity – 100 per cent of purchase price and cost of works funded

A client was looking to purchase a retail unit with office facilities above. The client needed to move quickly in order to secure the purchase at £325,000.

Once the property was purchased, the office above was turned into two flats and the commercial unit below was also split into two, to make the rental units more appealing to typical tenants in the area.

The client has a portfolio of properties which enabled 60 per cent funding (£195,000) to be secured on the new purchase with the balance (£130,000) and cost of works (£60,000) being secured on another property owned.

Once the flats were finished, these were valued at £165,000 each and both commercial units were able to have new seven-year full repairing leases (FRI) put in place at £1,000 pcm each.

The flats were refinanced over to long-term lending at 75 per cent (£247,500 raised) and both commercial units were funded with the same lender, with both commercial units valued together at £250,000 (a 60 per cent loan was taken for £150,000).

CASE STUDY

Get your ducks in a row early

One of my clients purchased a half-completed nine-bedroom HMO. The purchase price was £405,000 but the end-value after works was expected to be at the £550,000 level. After exchanging contracts, my client was directed to a large commercial lender whom she had quite a good track record with. The product recommended to her was a 75 per cent bridging loan, which on completion of the loan, would be converted into a long-term HMO mortgage at a new value.

My client had to pay an arrangement fee and survey fee for the bridging loan. However, the valuation for the bridging included the surveyor's valuation for the end-product after works were done. So, it was a two-in-one valuation. On completion of the works, the surveyor only had to go to the property to confirm that the works had been done as expected, and the value of £550,000 was now achieved. At that point, the lender moved the bridging loan onto a long-term product without a further arrangement fee. It was also a 75 per cent LTV product so that my client benefitted from a much higher loan advance, as the 75 per cent LTV was based on a higher £550,000 value. The arrangement fees were also saved on the remortgage. Such products work really well for properties that require refurbishment and where the investor wants to hold the property long-term. However, you need to work this out with your broker very early on as only a few companies offer a bridging product that can be converted into a long-term loan.

If you want to discuss your finance needs for your auction purchases, call Mortgage Desk on 01296 329610 or email fastfinance@mortgage-desk.com to find out how they can help.

CHAPTER 12
THE BIG DAY – BEST PRACTICE

@the.auction.insider The auction day is a unique experience. Each individual auction house will conduct the auction differently, which creates a more unique experience for the buyer. In order to make a success of the auction, you will need to take the following actions which will enable you to get the most out of the day.

AUCTION DAY CHECKLIST

This is a quick checklist of what you will need to have with you on the day of the auction to bid and exchange contracts quickly and smoothly.

1 **Register to bid:** In order to make a bid at the auction, you will need to register first. The registration process requires you to show that you have the correct and valid identification documents. You also need these in order to complete the memorandum of sale once you are successful with your bid; this is normally when you are presented with a unique bidding number (if applicable).

   i   Photographic identification: Traditionally this will be either a valid passport or full valid driving licence.

    ii   Proof of address: Most often required at the auction will be a bank statement/utility bill/council tax bill. This must be dated within three months of the auction and cannot be a mobile phone bill.

    iii If you are attending the auction to bid for another person, you will need to provide their identification (as above) alongside your own identification (as above) with a signed and dated letter of authority from the buyer, which authorises you to bid for them.

    iv If you are attending the auction to bid on behalf of your company (even for sole traders), you will need to provide the company's documents (certificate of incorporation) and identification of the director/shareholder (as above) who is the party of significant control, alongside your own identification (as above) with a signed and dated letter of authority from the company, which authorises you to bid for them.

These requirements are imposed upon all auctioneers and estate agents by HMRC, who are the industry regulators. This enhanced due diligence is in place to ensure that there is a clear understanding of who the buyer is, both legally and equitably.

2 **Solicitor's details:** I recommend coming prepared to an auction and this extends to having a solicitor ready in preparation for you to win the property. If you have already supplied and obtained advice on the legal pack, then it is appropriate to use that same solicitor to handle the completion for you. This will save time and money. If you

haven't taken that step prior to the auction, but you have a solicitor in mind, I would recommend contacting them in advance and asking them to open a file – this is a simple process, especially if you have used them recently. At the auction, every step you take should be proactive and put in place to save time and money.

3 **Funding/finance:** There are many ways to finance property in the modern age, some of which have been discussed in earlier chapters. There are however, opportunities to obtain finance at the auction. Most auctioneers will normally have a couple of auction finance providers in the room to assist potential buyers and winning bidders with their purchase.

4 **Method of payment:** It is worth checking with the auction house (details normally provided in the catalogue) which methods of payment they accept, before you attend the auction. Remember, on the day of the auction you will need to pay a 10 per cent non-refundable deposit (which can be subject to a minimum deposit) and the buyer's fee and buyer's premium where applicable. In general, the standard methods of payment can be:

i **Credit card/debit card:** This is possibly the most utilised method of payment on the day of the auction. Remember that you may have a daily limit and you will need to notify your bank/building society in advance of the auction to avoid a declined payment.

ii **Cheque:** These are still used at auction as a method of payment, although this seems to be dying out. Normally, a buyer will seek to gain access to the property between exchange and completion, and most sellers will refuse this if the funds have not yet cleared. People seem to be picking up on this and are choosing the other methods for speed, and to try and guarantee access to the property between exchange and completion.

iii **Electronic (same day) bank transfer:** This is one of the most efficient forms of payment on the day of the auction. As long as you have either online banking or telephone banking, you will be able to make an electronic transfer. This method of payment is fairly instant and not normally subject to a daily payment limit (you should check with your account provider before bidding).

MASTER THE AUCTION ROOM

There are ways to give yourself a competitive edge in the auction. Below, I have listed some things that I have done and that I have heard other auction professionals do. Their success is normally dependent on the size of the auction, and the shape and level of activity in the room. Success is also based on your ability to keep focus and most importantly, to pay close attention.

1 **Make sure that you have everything you need.** If you have followed the previous instructions, you should have with you a copy of the auction catalogue, the addendum, the late lots listings, your identification, payment method and

solicitor's details. Having that checklist completed means that you can focus effectively on the auction, the auctioneer and the other bidder.

2 **Location, location, location.** Picking a good vantage point in the auction is important for several reasons. First, it gives you an uninterrupted point of view, which enables you to clearly see the auctioneer and the other bidders. This is important, because you want to know who you are bidding against, and when the bidding is taking place you want to know whose turn it is to bid next. It is also important to find a comfortable place within the room as this will help you to relax in readiness for the bidding. To get your pick of comfortable spots in the auction, make sure you arrive early.

3 **Pay close attention.** There is always a lot going on in the lead-up to the auction. There will be a steady stream of other bidders coming and going, there will be approved service providers in the room, and there will always be an unforeseeable drama taking place either just before the auction, or as the auction progresses. All of these things will cause distraction. Importantly, before the auction commences, the auctioneer will stand and talk through the rules and procedure of the auction (this is normally interspersed with a joke or two) as well as a read-through of the printed addendum. There may also be a verbal addendum – this is normally a last-minute change to the property, or notification of the property's removal from the auction. The verbal addendum will be repeated prior to

offering the property under the hammer, but it is nice to have as much forewarning as possible. This will allow you to reconsider the amount of your maximum bid, or if the property you attended the auction for is not being offered, it will save you a wasted day.

4   **Have a plan and stick to it.** This is potentially the hardest part of the process for you to control. Knowing this, I normally set myself three bidding goals, or three resistance barriers. It means that I have not given myself the hard task of win or lose, I have given myself access and opportunity to succeed.

   i   **The Steal Price:** This is my hopeful purchase price, the one I commit to paper and hope to achieve if there are no other bidders who take part in the auction for the property. This is normally within 10 per cent of the guide price (above or below). It is worth mentioning that different auctioneers will take bids in a different way; it is a pure style over substance process, so it's best to attend the auction as a practice run to get used to a new auctioneer and their style.

   ii **The Ideal Price:** This is the price I'd be happy with and still consider the auction purchase a success. This is the price that works based on my due diligence and valuing of the property including all of my costs. Eight times out of ten, I will stop at this price, or maybe stop bidding after an additional £3,000–£5,000 above this price. This approach takes the pressure out of losing a property and the fear of overpaying for the property all in one.

iii **The Worst-Case Price:** I will normally take this step for maybe two in every ten properties I go and bid for. I tell myself it's not because I have created an emotional connection with the property, but sometimes this is the case. Fortunately, I only get emotionally invested in a property if I feel I can add significant value to it (this is normally hope value) and this really does make me commit to the project if I am successful.

If the property fails to sell at the auction, go back and re-calculate your best bid and approach the auction house again with a post-auction offer.

THE REMOTE BIDDERS

There are three types of remote bidders. To provide context to the bidding, it is important to understand what these are and how they are treated differently. I will also discuss how to set up these remote bids, in case you are unable to attend the auction, or indeed, if you prefer to bid from the comfort of your own home. I recommend that all remote bidders view the auction via the live-stream facility on the auctioneer's website.

1 **The telephone bid:** This is possibly the most common route of remote bidding. People tend to choose this route because it is the most flexible in terms of bidding, and it allows them to bid in real time at the auction. I know a lot of telephone bidders will disclose their maximum bid

amount based on the guide price. This still gives the bidder a degree of anonymity with their bidding on the day. The telephone bidding form is available for download prior to the auction and can be printed, completed and returned to the auctioneers within plenty of time for the auction (normally with a signed, blank cheque attached). If your circumstances change and you can no longer attend the auction with the day approaching, then you can download, complete, scan and send the completed document to the auction house, and transfer the deposit over (either by electronic bank transfer or card payment) to ensure you are authorised to bid in advance. (Please note that the same identification requirements apply to telephone bidding as are applied to bidding in person.)

2 **The proxy bid:** The proxy bidder is someone who is normally either travelling or in meetings on the day of the auction, and therefore unable to bid by telephone. In this instance, the remote bidder will have to disclose their maximum price. This is required in order for the auctioneer to bid on their behalf. This price remains undisclosed and is between the auctioneer and the proxy bidder. The same submission process applies to the proxy, as per the telephone bidding above. (Please note that the same identification requirements apply to proxy bidding as are applied to bidding in person.)

3 **The online bid:** Some but not all auction houses will have a facility available for you to bid on properties live on the day of the auction. This is different from the online auction

(which is to be discussed in a later chapter). In order to register to bid, you will need to submit your identification, personal information and contact details which are then verified. You will also need to submit your payment details, and if you are successful, the deposit and buyer's fees will be deducted. There is different online bidding software available and they can vary from auction to auction, so please make sure you understand how the specific auctioneer's online bidding system works in advance. My knowledge here is based on software that I have trialled and worked with.

THE CONTRACTS DESK

I have purchased no fewer than fifteen properties at auction over the years, and I have attended many, many more auctions than that. In addition, my official role on the day of the auction is the head of the contracts desk. This gives me a unique view of both sides of the desk – what to look out for and how to get the most out of it.

1 **Attitude:** It is important to present yourself in a good manner at the contracts desk, especially if you are looking to make the auction part of your investment strategy. The contract staff feed back to the valuer information about the buyers they have interacted with on the day of the auction. This may seem like a small thing, but it sets a good precedent for when you next approach the auctioneers

and may even raise your credibility when it comes to pre-auction exchanges.

2   **The paperwork:** The fall of the auctioneer's hammer constitutes a legal exchange of contracts. The paperwork is important because it gives you something to take away, and something to show for all of your hard work up to that point. The paperwork consists of a Memorandum of Sale with the Special Conditions of Sale attached (where applicable). The memorandum of sale will need to be signed and completed, with the deposit and buyer's fee being paid before you are permitted to leave the auction. Leaving the auction without completing the contract and providing your deposit puts you in full breach of your contract with the seller. This is an important step to get right. The auction staff will run through the memorandum with you, either completing it for you, or allowing you to complete it, if that is your preference.

3   **The deposit:** My main advice at the contracts desk is to prepare for things to go wrong (card payment declined, or pin code forgotten for instance), so always make sure that you bring with you a backup method of payment.

4   **Missing information:** It is important to have everything with you on the day of the auction. If you have missing identification documents, or missing solicitor's details (the most common), this will cause a delay in the exchange/completion process. The memoranda of sale cannot be sent out without this information; this means that neither yours nor the seller's solicitors have what they need to start the completion process. A delay on a twenty-day completion is

worrying, but a delay on a ten or fourteen-day completion is terrifying.

Preparation is the key to success at the auction and will benefit you greatly on the day. I do not recommend a 'winging it' approach here, nor do I recommend a lax approach to missing information.

THE SECRET AUCTIONEER LANGUAGE

I find myself attending a lot of property networking events and I also follow a lot of the property-specific Facebook groups/pages to help keep me up-to-date with changes in the market, as well as great networking opportunities.

There is a common theme that I find when attending these events and likewise when commenting on Facebook – there is a fear that 'you', the bidder will go to the auction, get carried away and overpay for the property.

This is a genuine fear and something that on occasion can happen at the auction. The important thing to remember is this:

Whilst the bidding is below the reserve price, the control over the room remains 90 per cent with the auctioneer, 5 per cent with the other bidders/onlookers and 5 per cent with you. Once the bidding exceeds the reserve price, 70 per cent of your actions during the bidding are influenced by the auctioneer, 20 per cent by the other bidders/onlookers and 10 per cent is within your own control.

Once you understand this, you are in a far better position to take back a larger percentage of control. There are of course professionals who have mastered bidding with greater control than the auctioneer, but for those who have not yet mastered this, or those who are looking to do so, below is my list of what to look out for:

1   **Speed and momentum:** Auctioneers require speed in the bidding to kick-start the momentum and then use that momentum for the following properties. To wrangle some of the control back from the auctioneer, change the pace of the bidding. You can draw it out (the most common method) or you can pre-empt a bid and potentially throw the auctioneer out of sync.

2   **Bidding increments:** The bidding increments are the main weapon of the auctioneer, used to ensure that the accruement of the bidding will hit the reserve price (as a minimum), rather than allowing the bidding to fall 'X' amount short of the reserve. A bid, if taken out of turn, can lead the final bid to be a single bid shy of the reserve. The true skill of the auctioneer is to manage the bidding and bid size to ensure that the reserve is met. So, do not be afraid to make a bid of a different increment to wrestle back some control.

3   **Competitor or chattel:** You may need to look twice, or you'll miss it. Sometimes an auctioneer, in order to gain momentum and to inspire other bidders to start bidding, can start a bidding war with themselves and a wall or light switch. This is only ever normally used to ignite existing interest and to make others in the room feel comfortable

with bidding. This technique obviously only works until the reserve is met by a third-party bidder.

4 **Stalling and goading:** Once the reserve has been met, the auctioneer may try some stalling when accepting a bid. This can be done to increase the anxiety in the room and unsettle the bidder and can also create time to allow another bidder to jump into the fray. The goading is normally light-hearted and jovial and is designed to spark the competitive nature of the bidders in order to extract an additional bid or two.

I hope these insights will give you far greater success and control over your bidding at the auction. Remember, the auctioneer has the final say in the room and as such, will always hold the lion's share of the control. However, there are ways to take back some control to level the playing field.

CHAPTER 13
IT'S NEVER TOO LATE TO BAG A BARGAIN

@the.auction.insider This is the chapter for all those who have either attended an auction and were unable to walk away with a property on the day, or those who either did not have the courage to attend the auction to bid, or whose strategy includes approaching unsold properties at the auction. Below is a guideline of how to approach a property/offer post-auction if you fall into one of the above categories.

THE UNFORTUNATE, THE UNLUCKY & THE PLAYERS:

1   The Disappointed Attendee (who failed to win the property on the day).
2   The Admirer from Afar (who lacked the confidence and conviction to attend to bid).
3   The Vigilant Opportunist (who is always ready to make an offer and never wants to lose out).

It is vital to know that your success with a post-auction bid is dependent on speed and certainty. This means that you will have already done the following as a bare minimum:

1   Read and understood the legal pack (or obtained legal advice on the contents).

2 Viewed the property (externally at the very least, but internally is preferable).

3 Have your finance and solicitor already primed and awaiting instruction.

You will need to strike whilst the iron is hot when it comes to post-auction offers, so be sure to ask the correct questions. Here are a few that I would recommend asking, in addition to any others:

1 It's a little obvious but ask if the property is still available. A lot can happen post-auction and websites can take a little while to update. So always ask to save yourself time and energy.

2 Do not ask for the reserve price! This is a fool's errand – if the property failed to sell, it clearly didn't meet its reserve. The better question to ask is, 'what is the strike now price?' Do not try and incentivise the seller with statements like, 'I'm a cash buyer' – the auction contract doesn't care, and neither do most vendors at auction. What does sometimes work is saying things like, 'I can complete earlier if needed'. This shows that you are a ready, willing and valid offeror.

3 The 'why'? Why is the seller selling – you are trying to find out if there is a problem to be solved, as well as whether there is some value to be added. It helps you to gauge the seller's attitude to selling and will help you approach the offer with elevated levels of success.

4 Ask for the memorandum of sale and bank details in advance of your offer being accepted. This shows an underlying desire to get the deal done and will combine strongly with your offer to the seller which may provide that additional motivation to accept your offer.

THE KNIGHT IN SHINING ARMOUR APPROACH

This approach is universal insofar as it applies to all three of the above categories.

The Knight in Shining Armour approach is the approach whereby the offer being accepted is made just in time to solve the seller's problem (which is normally connected to why they are selling in the first place). In this situation, you'll find that the seller is normally reasonable with the post-auction sales price and may be a little more flexible if, for example, you request an extended completion date.

This is one of the best ways I have seen people achieve success post-auction. It is very situational of course, but overall, it is a sturdy approach for post-auction offer-making.

THE WOLF IN SHEEP'S CLOTHING APPROACH

This approach is normally utilised by the vigilant opportunists (myself included, on at least two former occasions). This requires a very scattergun approach and, as such, can be very hit and miss. Its success can also be measured on how the market is functioning, as well as the seller's need for selling.

In this situation, you are not looking to solve a problem; you are mainly looking at acquiring a property at a price which is reasonable to you. The 'why' of the seller doesn't really matter too much here, because they will either accept your offer or refuse it.

Nevertheless, you need to present your offer in the same way as the Knight in Shining Armour. The main difference here is that your offer is likely to be a little to a lot lower than the seller's expectations and therefore requires further incentive:

1   Offer of quicker exchange and completion
2   Offer of assistance with selling fees

You are looking to make the seller's journey to making a decision easy, with as few barriers as possible. That is what makes this approach so successful.

THE FLEXIBLE FIXER APPROACH

I like this approach, because it isn't quite so much about the price you pay or the seller's 'why', it's about the property. You normally see this approach used for quite specific unsold property types:

1   **Land without planning:** This is where an intrepid and knowledgeable buyer would approach the seller with a JV (joint venture) opportunity. This is normally based on an added value basis at zero cost for the land. You will need to

secure the auctioneer's fees by way of a legal undertaking, but it is something that is becoming quite popular in recent years.

2   **Land with planning:** Like the above, but the difference here is not adding the value to the land by obtaining planning permission, but to actually build out the site. Again, this is normally done on a JV basis at zero cost for the land and with the auctioneer's fees secured via legal undertaking.

3   **The un-mortgageable property:** This can be anything from structural issues to having no kitchen, bathroom or roof fitted, and fire or water-damaged property. You would normally put down the deposit which is held to order, pending the completion of the works required to make the property mortgageable. You can then complete the purchase under the auction terms and conditions or turn to an end-user/owner-occupier.

4   **The paperwork purchase:** This is something that I normally see in relation to solving an issue such as:

   i   **Short lease flats:** Serving of section 42 notice prior to completion, the benefit of which is assigned to the incoming purchaser.

   ii **Enforcement notices:** Allowing the knowledgeable buyer to approach the local authority to make representations, defend or pay the fine off, and have the notice removed (this will need to be reflected in the purchase price).

THE PANICKED BUYER APPROACH

This is an approach that I normally see from the 'Admirer from Afar' category. This is normally seen with properties which are end-user/owner-occupier types of property, where the property values are fairly close to the perceived market value and, in most cases, being sold by end-user/owner-occupiers as well. This usually means that the purchaser has not seen the property in advance of the auction, nor read, or had the legal pack read, by a solicitor. This post-auction buyer will normally not proceed to exchange based on the above. Their motivation is normally quite low, and their timelines are not matched to those of the seller and the auction process in general. However, there is a select group who will proceed, and they do so quite blindly, which can make the completion problematic sometimes. This does not always affect the seller, but in some instances, it can do, so it is important for the panic buyers to be both vigilant and opportunistic. In order to do that, they should definitely interact with the auction process before the property fails to sell and to undertake to complete as much due diligence as possible. There is success to be had with this method, but it requires preparation.

Above are some of the approaches that I see on a regular basis. There are sure to be several others out there and you yourself may have your own way of approaching post-auction properties. What is important is to be authentic in your approach and to not be afraid to negotiate.

I HAVE THE POWER, NOW WHAT DO I DO WITH IT?

It is worth discussing the power shift post-auction. What I mean by this is the shift in negotiating power from the seller (pre-auction and auction day) over to the buyer (post-auction). In the post-auction scenario, the seller has seen their property fail to sell, or be withdrawn, or postponed, and are naturally disheartened.

This is where the Knight in Shining Armour rides in and saves the day. That is what makes it such a winning strategy, and likewise with the Wolf in Sheep's Clothing approach. Both approaches are relying on the seller being on one side or the other of the motivated/desperate line with their sale.

There is, of course, a sweet spot in the approach to a disheartened seller, and there are many ways to present yourself as the prime opportunity for disposing of the asset. This comes with a great degree of interacting with sellers (via agents and offers direct), experience, and through being a seller yourself. I normally work just below the reasonableness line. That means I look for the most reasonable approach to take, and then operate below that level. It is a very subjective thing to do, so make sure you have asked the right questions and conducted a full due diligence process.

Being slightly unreasonable makes you far more approachable than being completely unreasonable, and generally commands more respect than being either reasonable or too reasonable. You want to exercise your power responsibly, but also, you'll want to set the pace and have some more control over the transaction. Being slightly unreasonable offers you the potential to achieve this.

However, in all circumstances, there is a power shift. It is important for all parties to the transaction to be aware of this, and to take appropriate action in the transaction to secure a successful sale/purchase.

THE CONDITIONED OR THE CONDITIONER?

All sales at auction are subject to the common auction conditions of sale, unless varied by any special conditions of sale which may or may not be applied. Having said that, there are ways to negotiate in at least two of the three buying points at auction:

1   Pre-auction (negotiable)
2   Auction day (non-negotiable)
3   Post-auction (negotiable)

We have discussed pre-auction in a previous chapter, so we will focus on the post-auction process here. Now, although the processes are very similar, and, in most instances, identical, the approach is almost entirely different.

With regards to pre-auction offers, your ability to negotiate is mainly based on your offer represented as a price consideration only. With the post-auction sales, you are in a stronger negotiation position and, as such, you have the opportunity to apply or vary conditions to being 'the conditioner', rather than being 'the conditioned'. Below are a few conditions I have seen either varied, replaced, added or removed as part of a post-auction exchange:

1   The completion date being varied is the most common clause that I see being varied on post-auction transactions.

2   The contribution to sellers' legal fees is the most common clause that I see removed as part of the negotiation process.

3   The seller's cost of sale (separate from legal fees), represented as either a percentage of the sale or a minimum fee structure. This is normally replaced and is normally something that is borne 50 per cent by the seller and 50 per cent by the buyer.

4   Not as rare as some may think, I sometimes see a clause being added that allows the buyer to enter the property and commence works prior to the completion.

I have added the most common clause in each category, hopefully to highlight how common it is to negotiate (not just in price) more advantageous terms and conditions in a post-auction transaction.

CHAPTER 14
ONLINE AUCTIONS – PROP-TECH IN ACTION

@the.auction.pro Auctions are developing and, like most aspects of our lives, are influenced by new technology. Online banking is a standard for everyone; blockchain technology is trying to make an impact on how we transact, properties are funded by online crowdfunding platforms where thousands of people invest in a single deal, and emails, WhatsApp and video calls are changing the way we communicate. It's hard to imagine life without a mobile phone and a laptop, and now property technology is also expanding and helping us with finding properties, doing research, funding deals and selling.

The innovation is not in avoiding property auctions. There are lots of ways that auctions are being innovated and this chapter is going to shed some light on those.

Many people are familiar with the way eBay operates. You have something to sell, you list it online, get people to bid, the winner pays by PayPal and then a few days later receives the purchased item.

As discussed in the book, traditional auctions are referred to by many terms including 'in-room', 'traditional', 'ballroom style' and 'live', and they feature an auctioneer standing at the front of the room with a gavel (hammer) selling the property to the assembled public in front of him or her and over the phone.

Some auctions do take online live bids, but these are handled in the same physical way as any others.

The property is sold to the highest bidder, but physical factors often affect the sale, e.g. the number of bidders in the room, how busy the room is, geography and even the weather. You are also at the mercy of the skills of the auctioneer and, although they often appear superhuman, they can have off days like the rest of us. Sadly taking into account money-laundering aspects of the purchase and the purchaser is apt in this instance. The paperwork, financials, money laundering and auction contracts are all manually produced and, although the traditional room provides a spectacle for onlookers, there are many areas for human error which can affect the outcomes of the sale.

By comparison, online auctions cut out many of these human errors by using a computer system. The system has been designed to allow the same outcomes to be achieved as those in an in-room auction, using a combination of a website and the internet.

The other major choice for vendors is the differentiation between 'timed' and 'flexible'. A timed auction allows the auctioneer to collate a catalogue with a defined finish time. This is similar to the traditional route of providing a marketing platform for the agent to generate more interest, as there are more lots offered.

'Flexible', as the name suggests, allows the vendor to choose when the auction ends. This could be any time thanks to the advent of technology and for some lots, auctioneers have considered overnight endings due to the volume of overseas purchasers.

TYPES OF ONLINE AUCTIONS

Online property auctions are somewhat more complicated and not yet as established as eBay's technology. There are a few different formats that have grown from different backgrounds and they can be quite confusing. I will focus on the two most used ways of selling properties online.

MODERN METHOD OF AUCTION (CONDITIONAL)

This is a method that probably grew out of estate agents trying to leverage the excitement and results that the bidding process can produce. In the modern method of auction, properties are offered with a legal pack in advance of the auction. The auction is open for bidding for an extended period of time, normally about twenty-four to seventy-two hours. You get to view the property beforehand, and review the legal pack. When you bid and win, you are not exchanging contracts on the property. You are merely reserving the property at the given price and you are required to pay a reservation fee of about £6,000 inc. VAT. This is a fee to an auction company and does not form part of the purchase price or the deposit.

After reserving the property, you get about twenty-eight to fifty-six days to exchange contracts on the property. Again, you are not obliged to do it, but given that you have had to pay a £6,000 fee, it means you are likely to want to progress the transaction. The large window to exchange contracts is there to allow purchasers to arrange their mortgage or suitable finance. Only after you exchange contracts are you bound to complete the transaction – one to four weeks later, depending on the contract.

Modern methods of auction are much slower than the traditional auction. They allow purchasers to arrange finance that is cheaper than normal finance. I would go as far as to say they are just a light upgrade to a sealed bid process that estate agents used to use with popular properties. The upgrade also includes additional fees that the buyer has to pay on top of the purchase price. Normally, the fee is paid by the seller (unless added to special conditions), but here it's paid by the buyer by default.

I am not a big fan of the modern method of auction. It seems to be for half-committed sellers and half-committed buyers and the one getting the most benefit is the agent/auction house.

UNCONDITIONAL ONLINE AUCTION

This method of auction is extremely similar to the traditional auction, but with the exception that the bidding takes place on the online platform instead of in the physical room. The winning bidder has to pre-register, sometimes put a refundable deposit/commitment fee down, and the moment the bidder wins, the contracts are exchanged and the fee becomes non-refundable. If you were the underbidder, the deposit/commitment fee is refunded.

Online auctions have the benefit of even higher transparency, as your bidders cannot influence one another or try to intimidate each other. Hence the values achieved are expected to be much more realistic in terms of what the property is worth.

As with traditional auctions, the period of marketing matters a lot. The auction itself can take place over a one-day window, or a ten-minute window set by the auction house. The end time of the auction can be extended, almost indefinitely, by another minute if there is a bid placed in the last twenty or thirty seconds of the auction. This is to prevent people from placing 'sniper' type bids in the last seconds, and to allow others to respond to such last-second bids.

As with traditional auction, you will have to do the same kind of research, as the moment you win the bidding, you have exchanged contracts.

From my experience, online auctions are very good for smaller types of deals, between around £5,000–£100,000. People can be driven by curiosity and a sense of control/safety to bid more on properties in that region offered in the online auction.

I have sold three of my clients' properties in the online auction. Those were three sub-£20,000 flats in a small town in Wales.

Two properties were offered in the normal auction. They sold, but the buyer decided not to complete on them. So, we re-offered them in the online auction alongside another property that the neighbouring owner wanted to sell.

The two flats sold in the auction. Another sold just after the auction to a person who was interested in buying, but who had not been confident enough to bid in the auction.

The benefit of selling in the online auction in that example was that we did not have to wait for the next traditional auction, which was going to be in six weeks' time. The properties were marketed prior, so we could schedule an online auction within two weeks and by the time the normal auction took place, the transactions would have already completed.

THE PROS OF ONLINE AUCTIONS

1   More controllable
2   Generally faster
3   More cost-effective as you're leveraging technology
4   Less prone to human error
5   Familiar (as with the eBay method)
6   Better for buyers as they are more transparent

THE CONS OF ONLINE AUCTIONS

1   It is harder to establish trust as there is less human interaction
2   They are a new and unfamiliar concept, so are not as trustworthy
3   There are too many players who are not auctioneers, trying to make a quick buck
4   They are often confused with the 'modern method' of auction, which has major differences
5   Traditional auctions already have a big following

SELLER TIPS

1   Choose a company that has a history of holding auctions.

Estate agents with bolt-on auction systems are not as effective in the online field.

2   Ensure you understand how much the company is charging the buyer to purchase, as this can have a negative impact on the price you receive.

3   Give yourself enough marketing time. Often, sellers need money quickly and try to reduce the amount of time until the auction date. Unfortunately, this can impact the price dramatically, so I'd always recommend a minimum of three weeks if you can afford it.

4   Always allow viewings. Just because the auction is using an online engine, remember, the buyer is buying an asset or a home.

5   Use a solicitor who understands the auction process. Many say they do, but in reality, they only understand the normal conveyancing processes.

BUYER TIPS

1   Read and understand the legal pack before committing to purchase. Also, run it past a competent solicitor.

2   Have a survey carried out by an independent RICS surveyor, i.e. one not instructed by the seller's agent.

3   Always view the property.

4   Try to secure the property outside the process, i.e. do a deal with the auctioneer before, if you can.

5   If using a mortgage, always have an agreement in principle before paying the commitment fee.

UPDATES

This chapter is going to be out of date quite quickly, so we decided to devote a special section on our website to online auctions. That section will be updated regularly with new and up-to-date content, and it will help you to demystify online auctions.

Visit www.beforethehammerfalls.com/online-auctions

CHAPTER 15
SELLING IN AUCTIONS

WHY SELL IN AUCTIONS?

@the.auction.pro Auctions are a fantastic way to sell property. They have been around for years and have always been well-attended by professional property investors. Now, with the advent of *Homes Under the Hammer*, the general public, first-time buyers and amateur property investors have become more involved in auctions and driven the prices of some of the properties well beyond what many professionals would pay.

But the fact remains that the auction is a place where every investor who sees value in a given property can offer their best price at a given time. This accomplishes two things: the transaction is performed at its true market value (given appropriate marketing) and the transaction becomes effective immediately. What a great way to sell a property.

Once the gavel falls in the auction, the contracts are exchanged, and the parties normally have twenty working days to complete the transaction. This gives a lot of confidence to the sellers and buyers alike. The transaction is final at the fall of the gavel.

Auctions are a great tool to use to get interested parties in a property to actually perform. On several occasions,

I have helped investors who had offers made on their properties by interested buyers. Unfortunately, if there is no deadline, it causes the parties to engage in long and fruitless conversations. Auctions get rid of that. The seller sets the terms of the sale by way of auction contract and special conditions, and the buyers have to abide by it. Everyone is bidding on the same thing and they have a chance to put their own price tag on the property. The deadline set by the auction date creates tension and the risk for potential buyers that there will be someone else willing to bid above the reserve price and snatch the property from them.

CASE STUDY

Straight flip to a captive audience

One of my investors purchased a small office block in Wokingham, Berkshire. She bought it off-market through an architect introduction. The deal was good; the office had planning for three flats and she was confident she could get it upped to four flats. She did that, and exchanged contracts on the property with a delayed completion of three months. However, before completion, her preferred builder came up with a very high quote and, having other projects to manage, this one became a burden. My client looked to exit the project at cost of purchase — £480,000. She had it listed on a discreet basis with two local agents, but they weren't bringing any offers. I told her that properties like that usually fly in the auction, especially if the reserve is set at a reasonable level. I convinced her to put it in one of the London auctions that I thought was the most suitable for the location. The property proved so popular that it never made it to the auction. A flurry of pre-auction offers came in a couple of weeks into the marketing period, and my client chose to sell the property before the auction for a whopping £565,000, generating £85,000 profit on a property that she had been ready to exit at cost!

CASE STUDY

Competition effect

That same client had a very large eleven-bed HMO in Berkshire where the sale with the current buyer was prolonged. My suggestion to my client was to give the buyers a deadline upon which, if they failed to exchange, the property would be entered into an auction. My client followed my suggestion but the buyer continued to delay the exchange. She entered the property into the auction. One week following that, the buyer, knowing that the competition was mounting, found a newly-discovered enthusiasm for the purchase and exchanged contracts immediately. My client was only liable for marketing costs for the auction and a small pre-agreed withdrawal fee. The client was happy, and the buyer ended up performing. It was a win-win, but only because of the competitive environment that was created due to the auction hard-deadline.

TYPES OF PROPERTIES THAT SELL WELL

Auction sales tend to happen, in many cases, out of the motivation of the seller and their circumstances, such as a need for speed, confidence in the sale and transparency. However, if you are not forced to sell in the auction and you are considering various channels of sale, you might want to read this paragraph to give you an idea of what performs well in the auction.

If your circumstances force you to use auctions as a channel to sell, you can use this chapter to help you position your property as a potentially attractive lot and achieve a good price.

Auctions are usually a great place for selling:

1   Most properties in a bad or tired condition (expose your property to professionals, amateurs and end-users looking for a deal right now).

2   Land and oddly-shaped plots (let the market and people willing to put down the deposit decide what it's worth).

3   Income-producing assets that might have some issues (auctions are full of experienced investors who would not be afraid to take these on).

4   Properties with development potential (expose your property to people who can spot that and know how to navigate through the planning risks).

5   Leasehold properties with low leases (which can normally only be purchased by cash buyers).

6   Garages, unusual types of properties such as former water pumps, bunkers, ponds, woodlands, former public conveniences etc. (the auction is a perfect place for the market value of such products to be determined).

7 Properties where transparency is required.

8 Most of the properties where the reserve can be set at a very low level that attracts people to come to bid.

Auctions are not so great for other types of properties, i.e. beautifully renovated homes that need time to be appreciated. Usually with such properties, the buyers need time to appreciate various aspects and details of the property in order to pay the price that is being asked. It's not worth the risk of offering the property with a low reserve price and not giving people time to appreciate the value, because other types of buyers will definitely not pay the amount that an appreciative buyer would pay.

AUCTIONS VS ESTATE AGENTS

Auctions and estate agents follow two very different processes when selling properties. It's important to understand the principles on which they are both operating, as it will allow you to understand many other aspects of both worlds.

Estate agents, when appraising the property, usually try to be ambitious, offering to sell it at a price that is well above market value. This is done in order to win the instruction. After some marketing, the offers that come in are usually much lower than the marketing price and this is usually what gets agreed. If the marketing price is £275,000, then the possible selling price might be around £250,000. After the sale is agreed, the whole process of conveyancing starts and this could take anything from eight weeks to twelve months and more! The offers can be withdrawn at any time and both parties are free to walk away from transaction until the end of the conveyancing process, where the exchange of contracts happens.

Auctioneers work completely differently. Let's look at that same property that is worth £250,000, which the estate agent is trying to market at £275,000. The auctioneer would try to secure the reserve at around 15 to 20 per cent below the normal value of the property, based on recent sold prices of similar properties. So, in this example, the reserve would likely be set around £200,000–£220,000. In a tough market, in order to sell the property, the discount could be as much as 30 to 40 per cent of the recent sold prices, depending on the property and any potential issues that it might come with.

Once the reserve is set (let's assume it is set at £210,000), then the guide price would be set within 10 per cent of the reserve price. At the point of entering the property into the auction, the seller would be signing a binding auction contract which would have a clause covering withdrawal fees. It would say that in case of the seller wanting to withdraw the property from the auction, they would need to pay the agreed commission fee (around 2–2.5 per cent +VAT) on the reserve price as a penalty for doing so. The same penalty applies if the reserve is increased above the contracted level, and the property fails to sell at the auction. Both of those clauses ensure that sellers are committed to the process.

The property is marketed for about two or three weeks, potential buyers have an opportunity to review the legal pack and conditions of sale, and the auction happens on the set day giving everyone a chance to bid at the same time. Once the gavel falls, the contracts are exchanged, the 10 per cent deposit is paid by the buyer, and both parties now usually have four weeks to complete the transaction.

So, the auctioneer's job is to secure the property at the right level to attract interest, and to ensure the best chances of the property selling on the day of the auction rather than just taking an instruction to sell.

The commitment that is present in the auction environment dictates the price at which properties are valued.

CHOOSING THE RIGHT AUCTIONEER

Choosing the right auctioneer for your property is crucial. The various types of auctioneers that you can choose from include:

1   Local vs national
2   Online vs traditional
3   Large vs small/medium auction

The above considerations are typically best tackled by looking at what sold in the past in your area. This is best done using eigpropertyauctions.co.uk and searching for properties offered within a one-mile radius from your property.

Look at what has been sold, what has not been sold and the sale date. By looking at that, you will find the best auctioneers to go with.

Auctioneers who have sold properties in your area recently might be the best, since they have a database of people who had missed out in the previous auctions ready to buy.

Auctioneers who offered but did not sell or withdrew the property might still be a good bet if there are obvious reasons why this was so (such as the price being too high, obvious legal/structural issues, or other similar issues). It's good to at least have a conversation with these auctioneers.

Local auctioneers are typically good for properties that are new to the market and which haven't been offered before in the auction. There is a novelty element, and local people might want to jump on the opportunity.

National auctioneers offer their properties in the London auction. It does not mean that anyone wanting to bid has to come to London. Bidders can submit proxy bids, telephone bids and even bid online while the real auction is taking place. Distance does not have to be a barrier.

The best properties to list with national auctioneers are typically those that appear very attractive to the London buyers. These include high-yielding properties, development opportunities, and attractive and possibly unusual properties.

In the national auction, you can probably get away with a property that has been offered multiple times (given the right reserve price), as they have around 100–300 properties in one auction, and some people don't go into in-depth due diligence when buying. The benefit of the larger national auction will be that, due to the sheer volume of properties, your property will be carried through the reserve line much more smoothly than in a local auction.

Online auctions are typically good for lower-value pieces of land and low-value high-yielding properties (from experience: £100,000 and below). There is a lot of novelty to online auctions and taking risk on a low-value property does not seem to bother many potential residential buyers. However, the commercial auctions and buyers of commercial properties are also starting to fully embrace the online auctions element. There has been a recent online lot sale at over £5 million for a large piece of land in Manchester.

Selling a higher-ticket residential property is not such an easy thing, but there are some new online auctions entering the UK market that are having a shot at it. This is still a very new phenomenon in the UK – although in Ireland it took off over a decade ago.

Traditional auctions will still be the best choice for most sellers looking for a swift sale.

I tend to typically go for medium to large auctions with my sales. This is due to the fact that they have a much better coverage and there is always a possibility that some unsatisfied underbidder will just want to walk away with a property, therefore bidding blindly on your lot.

WHAT'S REQUIRED BEFORE ENTERING THE PROPERTY IN THE AUCTION

1 Positioning
2 Upfront costs
3 Commitment

There are normally some costs involved with entering a property for an auction. The main costs will include:

1 **Catalogue entry fee** (between £350–£1,000 depending on the size of the entry required).
2 **Solicitor costs.** Your solicitor will need to prepare a legal pack and a good solicitor will normally charge between £900 and £1,500 for preparing a legal pack. This will be needed well before the auction, as the buyers will need to make themselves comfortable with the contents.
3 **Cost of searches** (typically around £200–£400 – your solicitor will advise you). This cost is normally claimed back from the buyer as the searches are provided for their benefit.

Your property will need to be correctly positioned. An accurate catalogue entry is a good start, but it's also important to highlight the possibilities of the investment. Phrases such as 'development potential', 'refurbishment', 'first time on the market in X years' would get people's attention. Your auctioneer should be able to advise you on the best way to position your property but do make your own suggestions.

Solicitors play a crucial role in the auction sale. You are setting the terms of the sale in advance of the auction, and on the auction day, one of the bidders will be committing themselves legally and financially to fulfilling the terms of the sale. Your solicitor will need to ensure that your interest is protected, that the terms of the sale reflect what your expectations are, and that they are mitigating the potential risks you might face.

At the same time, your solicitor will need to prepare a legal pack that will answer the concerns of the potential buyer. The solicitor will need to put themselves in the shoes of the buyer and ask what kind of information the buyer will need in order to be confident in bidding.

In the auction sale, about 90 per cent of the solicitor's work goes into preparing the legal pack. The remaining 10 per cent is requesting the balance from the buyer's solicitor and dealing with the standard conveyancing matters that happen post-exchange of contracts.

DEALING WITH OBSTACLES AND NASTY OFFERS

When you enter a property into the auction at a fairly low price, you will be inviting people who don't understand the auction process to make silly offers for your property. It is best to let the auctioneer handle them for you. If the reserve price on your property is £220,000 and the guide price is £200,000, expect to receive some silly offers well below £200,000. This is what people who are not familiar with the auction process do. The auctioneer would normally filter such offers and set the expectations of such a person straight. But there might be times that such offers reach you, thereby shaking your confidence. Remember to trust the process. There will be other people who are doing their due diligence, spending time and money on solicitors and surveys, and they are committing themselves to bid on your property in steps; very small, but significant to them. That process is what makes auctions successful. You will only ever need two people to be committed to purchasing your property to appear in the auction room.

You will also need patience and a willingness to stay with the process in order to achieve the best price possible in the auction.

FREE AUCTION APPRAISAL

If you are looking for a free auction appraisal of your property, submit the details here: www.sold.property/auction.

UNSOLD PROPERTY: THE PLAN OF ACTION

Selling in the auction requires you to be prepared for the fact that your property might not sell in the auction. What do you do then?

It will very much depend on the circumstances and reasons for the lack of sale.

Were there enough people viewing the property? How many viewed it? How many downloaded the legal pack?

Was there a common complaint about the property from the interested parties?

Were there any restrictive special conditions, such as non-standard completion, excessive fees etc.?

Once you determine the reason, go back to the drawing board and have a chat with the auctioneer. There might have been people who were willing to do the deal, had one of the conditions been changed. Post-auction that might be much easier, but the power will be on the buyer's side.

If you have not received any satisfactory post-auction offers, you might want to consider reoffering the property again in the next auction with a reduced price. Sometimes I had a property that would not reach the reserve of £450,000 in September, but then when reoffered in October, it would attract bids and sell at £452,000! Auctions can be unpredictable.

You can also consider switching from one auctioneer to another. Sometimes it works wonders. But it is equally important to address the causes of the failed sale, whether that is price or marketing or legal issues.

A final consideration would be to switch the channel of your sale. Perhaps fixing the property and selling it through an estate agent is more suitable for the type of property or price level.

You can also use a free auction appraisal form and submit your proposal for me to look at. I can then advise you on the best course of action.

BONUS CHAPTER 1
THE UNDERWRITE OPTION – INCREASING YOUR BUYING POWER

@the.auction.insider I am really excited to be writing about underwriting. It is normally the last thing I talk about at speaking events and panel discussions. It normally gets quite a lot of attention and certainly the largest amount of follow-up questions.

I will begin this chapter by stating outright that the underwrite method is my go-to method of securing property prior to the auction. It is the perfect win-win option for any seller and any buyer. It is worth qualifying the above statement by saying that it is the perfect win-win on the proviso that neither party falls victim to greed or stupidity.

In simple terms, the underwrite is a profit share Joint Venture agreement, whereby the underwriter (buyer) promises to buy the property at a fixed price prior to the auction and pending the outcome of the sale. I will run through the most common scenarios with an underwritten property below.

SCENARIO A: LOW RISK, INSTANT RETURN

The property is underwritten for £250,000 prior to the auction. The property sells at auction to a new party for £300,000. In this scenario, the property sells to the winning bidder at the auction. At the point of completion, the seller and the underwriter will split the difference between the underwritten price and the sales price. The allocation for the profit split is normally 45 per cent to the seller, 45 per cent to the underwriter and 10 per cent to the auction house (sometimes it can be a straight 50/50 split, auction dependent). In this scenario at 45 per cent, 45 per cent and 10 per cent, the seller gets £22,500, the underwriter gets £22,500 and the auction house gets £5,000. The underwriter is then refunded their underwrite deposit and buyer's fee, as well as the underwrite profit.

This is the simplest, most straightforward and unfettered underwriting approach. Here, you can see that the underwrite was triggered at the point of completion and not at the point of exchange. The reason for this is that the underwriter is under a promise to buy the property unless another party completes on the purchase. Another point to note is that the underwriter's deposit remains non-refundable until the new party actually completes on the purchase.

CASE STUDY

@the.auction.pro *There was a beautiful building offered in a commercial auction. I really liked the look of it, the numbers, and the potential it offered. I was also familiar with Aberdeen, having spent four years there at university.*

The building was let to Scottish Police at c. £120,000 pa, but the lease was due to expire about seven months after the auction. There were also two vacant shopfront units.

The building was in a great location, right in the centre of Aberdeen and very close to Marischal College.

The guide price was £500,000 and having done our due diligence, we were prepared to purchase it for £600,000 with a view to either extending the lease with Scottish Police, or developing the building into a residential, mixed-use or serviced accommodation/office unit. The possibilities were endless.

We managed to agree an underwrite at £600,000. It was not a bad price considering the seller had bought the building for £2.2 million in 2007!

The property went into the auction and sold for £675,000. Less than what we hoped for, but at the same time, we made £37,500 gross profit.

After deducting the solicitor's costs, planning consultant costs and other incidental costs, our profit was around £32,500 in only six weeks!

SCENARIO B: LOW RISK, PROPERTY ACQUIRED

@the.auction.insider The property is underwritten for £250,000 prior to the auction. The property sells at auction to the underwriter at the underwritten amount of £250,000. In this scenario, the property sells to the underwriter and the underwrite is triggered.

This is quite possibly the second-best outcome for an underwritten property. It too is a very straightforward and unfettered outcome from an underwritten property. Here, there is no profit split and the promise to exchange is exercised.

CASE STUDY

@the.auction.pro *The property was a two-bedroom flat on a pleasant council estate in Camberwell. With the guide price initially showing at £250,000 plus, we did an underwrite at £280,000. Flats in good condition in the same block were selling for as much as £380,000.*

We knew that this flat needed about £25,000 spent on it to refurbish it to a good standard. The reason it was cheap was because it had a tenant paying only £11,000 pa, who had been staying in the property for the past eight years. This was an issue that would put many people off from bidding. However, after reading the special conditions, we realized that the flat was going to be sold with vacant possession on completion.

We decided that at £280,000, it was a very good deal and proceeded with the underwrite. It turned out we were the only bidders for this property in the auction, and we ended up buying it. Just before completion, we went to visit the property to ensure everything was as it should be in order for us to complete. Once there, we realised that the tenant was not planning on moving out. We kicked up a legal fight with the seller's solicitor to have the property made vacant. Not only did we want to evict the tenant — there was a family of about eight people living in this two-bedroom flat! It was not something we wanted to handle.

The seller's solicitor admitted they had made a mistake in writing the special conditions, but tried to argue that it did not matter, as the property was advertised as tenanted. We did not accept that argument but knew it would take us a long time (and a lot of money) to fight it in court. Instead, we came to an agreement that we would pay an extra £10,000 to the seller and only complete when the property was vacant. It took the seller eight months to get vacant possession, but it allowed us to arrange a mortgage to complete on the property. It saved us about £10,000 in the finance costs so, after all, the extra cost was neutralized.

We refurbished the property in three months and put it back on the market. Because of the time it took us to complete (nine months from the auction!), the prices in the area increased, and we sold the property at £403,000 within another three months, making a substantial profit.

SCENARIO C: MILD RISK, DISCOUNT LEVERAGED

@the.auction.insider The property is underwritten for £250,000 prior to the auction. The property sells at auction to the underwriter for £300,000 (you want to own the property). In this scenario, the property sells to the underwriter at the auction. At the point of completion, the seller and the underwriter will split the difference between the underwritten price and the sales price. The allocation of the profit split is normally 45 per cent to the seller, 45 per cent to the underwriter and 10 per cent to the auction house (sometimes it can be a straight 50/50 split, auction dependent). In this scenario at 45 per cent, 45 per cent and 10 per cent the seller gets £22,500, the underwriter gets £22,500 and the auction house gets £5,000.

This is an approach that I have only seen work properly in scenarios where the underwriter genuinely wanted to own the property. If your approach is blatant profiteering with no real desire to own the property, then this approach is fraught with danger. In this scenario, because the underwriter won the property at the auction for a higher amount, they will be entering into a new contract (outside of the underwrite agreement) and therefore will need to provide a secondary deposit in order to exchange the contract.

As with Scenario B, once the property completes at the £300,000 price, the underwriter is then refunded their underwrite deposit and buyer's fee, as well as the underwrite profit. Their purchase of the property at £300,000 is in fact representative of a purchase price of £277,500, which is the purchase price net of the underwrite deposit. In this scenario, the underwriter has leveraged their buying position with a 45 per cent discount on every pound spent above the underwritten price.

This process can be abused by a reckless underwriter, or where greed takes hold and all common sense and reason is left by the wayside. Truly, only consider Scenario C if you are willing to own the property at the purchase price (obviously net of the underwrite profit).

CASE STUDY

@the.auction.pro *A nine-bed HMO came up in the auction. It was advertised as having a potential income of £66,000 pa, which I knew was not possible. £55,000 was the number we* were confident of. The property had a guide price of £375,000+ and we agreed an underwrite at £400,000.

We knew that we could have the property renovated and furnished for £50,000. It would revalue at £550,000 with the income at £55,000 pa, so we were confident purchasing it at up to £420,000 with the purchase price.

However, having underwritten it at £400,000, it meant that any amount over £400,000 would receive 45 per cent of uplift above that. So, for us, bidding up to £420,000 meant that we would receive 45 per cent of £20,000 back. In effect, the property would really cost us £411,000, giving us an advantage over other bidders.

We managed to win the bidding at £410,000, meaning the property cost us £405,500 after our underwriting profit.

However, bidding in the auction above the underwriting price and winning at that price created a new contract. The first contract is underwriting the lot at £400,000 – that required a £40,000 deposit. The second contract was the purchase contract at £410,000 that required another deposit of £41,000. If we failed to purchase the property under the purchase contract, our underwriting contract would step in and we would be required to complete under that contract. It potentially meant having lost two deposits!

Bidding above the underwriting price is not for the faint-hearted and requires you to be able to come up with a second deposit if you win the bid.

SCENARIO D: HIGH RISK — A WARNING

@the.auction.insider The property is underwritten for
£250,000 prior to the auction. The property sells at auction to
the underwriter for £350,000 (you got carried away). In this
scenario, the property sells to the underwriter at the auction. At
the point of completion, the seller and the underwriter will split
the difference between the underwritten price and the sales
price. The allocation for the profit split is normally 45 per cent
to the seller, 45 per cent to the underwriter and 10 per cent to
the auction house (sometimes it can be a straight 50/50 split,
auction dependent). In this scenario, at 45 per cent, 45 per cent
and 10 per cent the seller gets £45,000, the underwriter gets
£45,000 and the auction house gets £10,000.

This is an approach that I have yet to see work for an
underwriter, in a situation where greed got the better of them,
or they just got carried away. If your approach is blatant
profiteering with no real desire to own the property, then this
approach is fraught with danger. In this scenario, because the
underwriter won the property at the auction for a far higher
amount, they will be entering into a new contract (outside of
the underwrite agreement) and therefore will need to provide a
secondary deposit in order to exchange the contract.

As with scenario C, once the property completes at
the £350,000 price, the underwriter is then refunded their
underwrite deposit and buyer's fee as well as the underwrite
profit. Their purchase of the property at £350,000 is in fact
representative of a purchase price of £305,000 which is the

purchase price, net of the underwrite deposit. In this scenario, the underwriter has leveraged their buying position with a 45 per cent discount on every pound spent above the underwritten price, but has priced themselves out of most, if not all, of the profit at the point of exit. I have seen this cause issues with raising finance (if required) post exchange of contracts.

The underwrite for me is a brilliant method to access properties prior to the auction without taking the competitive bidding element away from the seller, and has the potential to return almost instant profits or, at the very least, offer a percentage of leverage between the underwritten price and the purchase price, if you as the underwriter win it at the auction for a higher amount.

If it sounds too good to be true, here is where it can all fall down (depending on mindset and intention). I have mentioned above that the underwrite profit, deposit and buyer's fees are retuned when the winning bidder completes on the purchase. Now if the winning bidder at the auction fails to complete, then the underwrite agreement is triggered and you exchange at that point. Remember, this is the very reason why the seller has agreed to potentially split an uplift for you. You are the guaranteed buyer.

Now if you are cunning, and you are thinking (as in scenario D) 'I have paid too much for this at the auction. I made a mistake and got carried away', you may decide to fail to complete at the £350,000 price and wait for the underwrite at £250,000 to kick in. This is not to be considered — the failing to complete at the higher amount will constitute a material breach of contract and may open you up to litigation, either in specific performance of the contract or a claim of detrimental loss.

I have seen this happen and it is not worth your consideration. There is no need to mess with something that is genuinely designed to be a win-win for all concerned. Any abuse of the underwrite comes with very specific and actionable consequences. I sincerely hope that I have scared you sufficiently on this subject.

BONUS CHAPTER 2
THINKING IN REVERSE – THE EXIT STRATEGY

@the.auction.insider For me, the important part of being a property professional is in being part of a journey. There are two types of journey that I get excited about:

1   My journey as a property professional. This encompasses continuing to learn and understand property, and property transaction from an arm's-length prospective. This applies to my own property investments and building a property portfolio.

2   The journey of each and every single property I interact with. This encompasses properties at the auction, my own properties, and living vicariously through other investors and their properties.

Every person is on a journey, and every single property form part of that journey. But the property is a journey in and of itself. In this bonus chapter, we are going to explore the importance of knowing the destination before the journey can begin.

The destination is important so you can avoid getting lost along the way. Property can be fun, rewarding, challenging and problematic. It is important to set yourself a roadmap — and I find starting at the end offers the most amount of clarity and foresight by setting intuitive goals.

I start each property transaction by asking myself the following questions. This helps me to divine the most appropriate exit strategy:

1   Why this property?
2   How does this property further my journey?
3   What am I looking to achieve?
4   Am I ready?

These questions seem fairly simple, and for the most part they are, but what this does is it makes you ask the question and take stock of the answers. It has prevented me from making silly mistakes in the past, especially when I was too quick to act, rather than engaging my brain and instincts.

Finally, before I really start to consider the exit too formally, I investigate the what if question which is attached to every property transaction in a good, bad or unremarkable market. I use this as a method to address potential risks, and then follow the exit strategy which mitigates those perceived risks, whilst being profitable and exciting.

THE PRICE FALLACY

This is likely to be controversial, so I'm just going to say it. The price that I pay for the property is not my first consideration when purchasing. My first consideration is:

how much will my buyer be willing to pay for this property as it stands today, then six months from now, then twelve months from now and finally two years from now? This forms my worst-case scenario, my cut and run position (especially in the short term). I have only had to use this exit once, in 2009, and I have been fortunate enough not to have had to use it more often than that.

All my other exits rely either on capital appreciation forecast, yielding asset calculation, or of course, added value (physical or paperwork) strategies. This principle relies on you eventually selling the property you have purchased. There are many out there who have no intention of selling, which is also fine, because the price you pay means even less — you cannot technically make a loss if you never realise (sell) the asset.

KNOWING ME, KNOWING YOU

Whilst it is vitally important to know why you are buying the property and what you intend to do with it, it is even more important to know why your buyers are going to buy your property. Most of what I am looking to achieve is to take unmortgageable properties and make them:

1 Mortgageable — for my buyer
2 Valuable — for my buyer
3 Saleable — for me

I am almost always looking at what will attract a buyer to my property and what will make it the most approachable property on the market within a half-mile radius.

I know what I am capable of. I know where I need to improve myself and I know where those two things fail to meet, so I have a list of trusted professionals that I work with to ensure that my failings do not affect the property journey, and that the 'ideal buyer demographic' has access to, and interest in, what it is that we have brought to the market.

I try where possible to consider the following when purchasing a property. This allows me to look beyond what I am trying to achieve and provides me with some insight into what my potential buyer is looking to achieve.

1   Who is my buyer?
2   What type of property are they looking for?
3   Where do they sit in the market?
4   Why are they my target buyer?
5   How best do I access them?

The answers to these questions enable me to tailor my exit strategy to fit my ideal buyer. As discussed previously, this isn't always the most profitable route (it may be the quickest for example). It is the route that means that I am achieving my goals, whether it be a quick in and out, a hold and never let go, or a high-yielding asset.

THE EGG TO BASKET RATIO

This consideration allows me to look at my existing property stock and gives me an opportunity to assess my risk and exposure levels. Generally, what I am looking for here is to see if I am overexposed in one of the following categories:

1   **Geographical area:** Following my experience of the 2007/2008 property crash/recession, I like to own properties in several different areas. I was slightly caught out in 2009 with three properties within a three-to-five-minute drive from each other. The convenience of the proximity of each property became less important, as this area fell by 10 per cent in the first twelve months and then 7 per cent in the following twelve months. The neighbouring area, however, saw a price drop of 6 per cent. After this (not too) painful experience, I no longer try to buy for geographical convenience.

2   **Property class:** I have no real negative experience with regards to having too much of one specific type of property in my control at any one point, but I do like the idea of a diversified portfolio and the spread of risk through different property classes. At the point of writing this book, I have a block of eight flats in Shropshire, and a commercial unit with planning potential in Runcorn under my control. My next buy, whilst retaining the two current properties, would be a short-lease flat (requiring refurbishment), which I always find fun to work on. I enjoy the different skills and knowledge required to work on each of these deals, which is

normally why, at any one point, the investments under my control will have different features.

3 **Price vs value:** At the moment, I am looking at maintaining a purchase price per unit in the £75,000–£150,000 range. This will of course change, as I normally like to own property at different price levels. However, the current market tells me that I still need to transact, but I do not want to overexpose myself in terms of capital at risk. The end value of the commercial unit will have paid for the unit and returned that initial investment back one and a half times over. This approach enables me to be nimble in the market, which for me is paramount.

Considering these points means that I can measure my risk of exposure to the mid to long term, which is where I operate. If I was looking at the short term, my primary consideration would be purchase price in relation to perceived market value.

HOW MUCH DO YOU SEE?

I was giving a talk in Q3 of 2018 to a fairly diverse group of investors and developers (mainly developers) and I had spoken about exit strategies with them. I highlighted the following principle of market/acquisitional sight, which I share here.

1 **Insight:** This is the ability to understand the true nature of something, normally achieved with the application of intuition and logic.

2 **Hindersight:** This is when you allow a past and often negative experience to prevent you from taking any further action.

3 **Foresight:** This is the ability to predict either what will happen in the future or what steps will need to be taken to achieve a specific goal.

4 **Hindsight:** This is the ability to only really understand what has happened after the event has taken place. It is why reflecting on a property transaction is important for growth and experience.

It is not simply a matter of knowing what you are doing or how you are going to do it — it is a matter of why, and more importantly, it is a matter of purpose. Having a strategy for investment enables you to act in a certain way. Implementing knowledge and experience enables you to act more fluidly. Stress-testing your approach in order to restrict uncertainty offers a degree of stability within a purchase. Accounting for multiple exits under a stress test to ensure a profitable destination creates comfort, and alleviates unnecessary stress associated with the 'what if?'

THE CONSIDERED APPROACH

1 Prepare a list of potential exit strategies (I have provided my top three at the end of the chapter).

2 Start with the primary exit in place (this can be changed at a later date, so do not worry).

3 Constantly monitor the progress of the transaction (see if any of the fundamentals have changed and adapt [or prepare to adapt]).

4 Monitor the marketplace for real or sentiment-based changes (this may change your buyer demographic or the market value).

5 Ready plan B (start considering plan C).

6 *Optional step* – ready your three (minimum) backup exits now.

7 Do not be afraid to change the priority of your exits. This is a situational part of the process (my primary consideration is exit with greatly reduced risk).

8 Completion day (even at this stage, do not be afraid to reconsider the exit).

9 Reflect and go around again.

With regards to the above steps, it is important to remember two things. First, analyse, but not to the point you restrict yourself from action. Second, there is plenty of time during the journey to measure and reassess your exits.

MY TOP THREE EXIT STRATEGIES

PLAN A – ADDED VALUE APPROACH

This is my one-size-fits-all approach and works best for the following investments. It is nimble and speedy once you are practiced.

1   Large flats (one or two beds) where the reception room and
    kitchen are separate (freeholder consent dependent). It is
    possible to convert the kitchen into another bedroom and
    make the reception room open plan with a new kitchen.
    This is added value, not just based on the additional
    bedroom, but with the new kitchen in place you have double
    the added value by carrying out a singular action.

2   Light refurbishment for me is tried and tested. It is not
    a stand-alone approach, but normally part of the other
    strategies I take. Sometimes (like in probate sales) it will
    allow me to add all the value I need for a speedy turnaround,
    just by making the property approachable to a far wider
    market place.

3   Rent review is something I look at, primarily with
    regards to my commercial purchases. I do pick up some
    underperforming assets and can quickly revitalise them
    with a simple paperwork exercise and then re-sell at a
    higher yield.

PLAN B – THE LONG HAUL

I like to take this approach when I have the time and capacity
to really work the asset. This normally takes a little more
time and can increase the risk vs reward ratio, but for me
(importantly), it's fun.

1   The two-storey maisonettes offer a great deal of potential
    to split into two separate flats. This requires a ready and
    willing freeholder and the creation of a new lease. You'd

be surprised how many freeholders like this approach. It requires a lot of up-front negotiation, but the benefits are all there. This only really works on the three-to-four-bed maisonettes in my experience.

2   The semi-detached or detached three-bedroom house offers great potential for splitting into self-contained flats. Depending on size and layout, I would normally go for a split into either two two-bedroom flats, or three studios (planning permission and works to the roof space may be required).

3   Planning gain on commercial property seems to be a real hot topic at the moment, but it is a valid exit strategy for me to consider. I prefer the secondary or tertiary parades, as these are normally surrounded with residential houses/flats and are normally far more affordable (at least on a £ per ft^2 calculation). On occasion, I will use this strategy in line with the rent review strategy which, again, can offer me a double-down on added value.

PLAN C – SPEED AND CERTAINTY

Depending on the purchase price and the perceived discount from market value, I will normally consider the auction. It is possible that I would have instigated one of my added value strategies already and will use the auction for a quick sale to enable me to move on to the next opportunity.

1   This is another one size (almost) fits all strategy. However, this is very much asset class and purchase price dependent.

2   Suitable properties for me include – short-lease flats, sites with potential for planning gain, rent reviews and

extension/conversions (not always doing the works, sometimes just obtaining the permissions).

3   Hope value – sometimes all this entails is pointing out the angle that you were going to pursue and let someone else cost in the hope value of achieving this. Sometimes it requires actual work in order to highlight/support the assertion of the hope value.

It is hoped that this bonus chapter has given you a short taster on the ways I look at properties and how I consider a multiple exit strategy.

BONUS CHAPTER 3
PREPARATION IS YOUR KEY TO SUCCESS

@the.auction.insider In this chapter, we are going to address what primary steps you should be looking to take if you want your property auction journey to be simple and with as little stress involved as possible. Specifically, we are going to talk about due diligence, connected services, leveraging your purchasing power, considering unforeseen costs and discussing your exit strategy.

DUE DILIGENCE

I imagine that I have possibly seen the full gamut of a potential purchaser's due diligence when considering their auction purchase. These range from the downright fear-inducing impulse buyers, all the way up to the ex-financial analyst with their colourful spreadsheets and stress tests. In the middle, we range from the ultra-cautious to the daring and the brave, and hidden in the middle of all the chaos, you'll find the problem solver.

In this section, I will highlight the starting blocks to becoming a problem solver. I will be focusing on this method of due diligence because it is the approach that I take and the approach I have seen used on many occasions with great success.

248

My first approach to any property would start by asking myself the following, which will determine whether I will be progressing with my due diligence process or not.

1   Does this opportunity fit in with my investment strategy?
2   How will I structure my purchase?
3   What am I looking to achieve from this property?

The following basics of due diligence are not designed to be one-size-fits-all but will highlight potentially unforeseen issues and/or may cause you to ask vital fact-finding questions. The aim of due diligence is to reduce risk and to qualify appropriate properties for purchase.

DESKTOP DUE DILIGENCE

This is always my first step in my due diligence process. It is structured and easy to action. This is the first point in my consideration that will allow me to confidently dismiss potential investments in the first instance, which saves time and energy. Most importantly, it allows me to focus on those properties which are far more suitable.

1   **Postcode search and Google street view.** I like to look at the street scene if I am not local, and especially if I am not overly familiar with the local area. A basic postcode search will bring up information relating to the local area. I like to see what the property is proximate to: local

schools, public transportation, other local shops and amenities.

2   **Property search: Rightmove, Zoopla, EI Group and Net House Prices.** I use these online searches (both sales and lettings) to see how active the local market is, to seek comparable properties to the one that I am considering, to look at similar properties that have sold on the same road within the last ten years, and to see if any other properties on the same road or neighbouring roads have been entered to auction.

3   **Planning portal search.** This may not be a relevant search for the property I am looking at, but in the first instance, I like to check if there is any lapsed, current or refused planning on the property. In the second instance I look to see which neighbouring properties have successfully gained planning and if that has set a precedent for the road, and if that same (or similar) permission could apply to the property I am scrutinising.

4   **Public register of enforcement notices.** I find myself checking this register purely out of habit, although it has provided me with useful insight in the past. I would recommend this search if you are looking at any property, but certainly use it without fail in all the following instances: HMOs licenced or otherwise, houses converted into flats, self-contained or otherwise, roof extensions and properties extended under permitted development.

5   **EPC register.** There is so much information to be gained from this exercise. First, I am looking to ensure that there

is an up-to-date EPC for the property on the register. Second, I am interested in the size of the property and finally, in the EPC rating itself. This tells me if the property is mortgageable and tells me its size (although this is not gospel, it is a good first indication).

6   **LHA rates.** I use the LHA rates when I am looking at properties which are already let and yielding. Before I approach local letting agents, I like to see if the current rent is: achievable and realistic to maintain long term with room to increase, if the property is under-let and what the local authority would pay as a worst-case scenario.

7   **Pound per square foot calculation.** I like to consider the £ per ft^2 calculation on everything I look at. It is especially useful for vacant property and developments (not so much tenanted property due to the existing yielding nature), but I do find myself checking the calculation out of habit. Even if the property looks to be good value on a yielding investment, I will check the £ per ft^2 calculation to make sure that I am not overpaying in capital for a yielding investment.

ADVANCED DUE DILIGENCE

Once a property has made it past the first level of due diligence, I scrutinise it further using the following steps. This section of due diligence may require some expenditure and may consume more time than the first section, but if a property makes it past this section, then it's one I will place a bid on at, or before, the auction.

1 **The drive-by.** I have discussed the importance of attending the open house viewings in another chapter and now reference this section as a reminder of its importance. The drive-by is potentially your first face-to-face interaction with the property. This means you'll be approaching the asset with fresh eyes, so make the most of it.

   i Look at the property, and I mean really look. I like to use the top to bottom approach. Roof — are the tiles uniform and in place? Does anything look loose? Does it look like any of them have been replaced recently? The pointing and brickwork — is anything loose or cracking? The windows — are they new? Are there any gaps, and are they secure?

  ii Look at neighbouring properties. You have already gone through the trouble of looking at the planning portal, now is your chance to see what has been put into action and look at elements of another person's hard work that you could capitalise on.

 iii Look at the street scene. How are the gardens and fascias of the neighbouring properties kept?

  iv Look at its proximity to local shops and services. Depending on the property and my exit strategies, I will be considering the following, all with varying levels of importance: schools, transport links (time travelled to reach the nearest local hub), supermarket and local conveniences (high street).

   v Look at the neighbourhood demographic. Depending on my exit strategy, I will consider who my tenants will be living next to and amongst, or who will be buying the property from me (owner/occupier). I want to know who lives there and who may want to live there. This will help with my pricing and estimate of my exit price. Always do two external visits to the property before attending the open house viewings or in conjunction with an open house viewing. I like a weekday between 5 p.m. and 7 p.m. and a weekend (normally a Saturday) between 11 a.m. and 2 p.m. I find that these are normally the most active times of the day and provide greater insight into the area and its inhabitants.

2 **The legal pack.** Before I hand the legal pack off to the solicitor, I like to check it myself (a legal dictionary is cheap but useful). I check it first, so that I can make my first line of enquiries to the auction house. I take note of every document that is there, and even more importantly, I take a note of what isn't there.

I then ask the auction house for any other documents that I feel are outstanding. This is most often a management pack for a leasehold property, a local authority search for a freehold property, or an environmental/water and drainage search for a development/potential development site. I have provided a short list below, but for further information, refer to the previous chapters.

I find myself paying careful attention to the special conditions of sale (may also be referred to as 'Contract', 'Auction Contract' or 'Common Conditions'). This document will form the primary foundation of your exchange and is arguably the most important document. Here are some of the reasons why:

i   The special conditions of sale will contain clauses that have varied the common auction conditions (RICS 3rd or 4th edition). If you are not aware of the common auction conditions, I'd recommend becoming familiar with them, if buying and selling at auctions is going to be part of your investment strategy.

ii   The completion date and/or the length of the completion are normally set out or confirmed in the special conditions of sale. This is very important, especially if it specifies a shorter completion date.

iii   Additional fees can be added to the special conditions of sale. These normally refer to a contribution towards the seller's solicitor fees and/or allocate the cost of the searches to the buyer.

iv   If the property is tenanted, there can be clauses in relation to apportionment of rent or payment of rent arrears. It is important to know what these costs are.

There are so many other examples, but the above are the ones I look for first and those that would impact my decision-making process the greatest. A good solicitor however will be able to draw your attention to the above and more, and as such, are worth their weight in gold.

3   **The local agents.** I like local estate agents because I like professionals who know their area and who provide a good level of quality service (granted that's not all agents, but this applies to the majority).

I usually approach three high street estate agents. I do like to use at least one independent estate agent in that mix (I wish I had a good reason for that, but it appears to be habit for me) and I will discuss the property with both the sale and letting departments.

I find myself asking the same set of questions of them all:

i   If I was to sell this property through you, how much would you market it for if I told you that I would want a queue of people outside your office wanting to put down a deposit within the first seventy-two hours?

ii   If I was to put the property up for rent with you, how much would you market the property for if I told you that I would want a queue of people outside your office wanting to put down a deposit within the first thirty-six hours?

iii   What are your fees?

It is a simple set of questions and an equally simple set of answers, but this can tell you a lot about the local market and about the potential cost (in part) for one of your exits. It's all very good looking at the sold prices in the area, but if that property sits on the market for four to six months before achieving that price, then that will affect your holding cost, finance and exit strategy.

CASE STUDY

The following case studies are real, but the names and addresses have been changed to protect all parties concerned. The general facts remain.

Example A: *The seller enters an unusual property into the auction. The property consists of a mid-terrace house, split into five letting rooms over three floors. The property does not benefit from an HMO licence and the tenure being offered for sale is the remainder of a twenty-year commercial lease. The property is on the market with a disclosed guide price of £150,000 and is producing approximately £55,000 per annum. The rent payable to the landlord is approximately £30,000, providing a net annual income of £15,000.*

The property is located just outside of prime central London in a popular north west London postcode. The property was popular with all in the room and sold on the day of the auction for approximately £180,000.

On the day of the auction, the buyer attended with no intention to purchase a property. However, they saw the postcode and the income and thought nothing more of it.

The buyer failed to complete their purchase. They had lost their deposit and costs exceeding more than £20,000 and were liable for losses and costs incurred by the seller because of their failure to complete.

This case study highlights perfectly the importance of due diligence. If anyone is curious about the property above and would like to know more about these complications or similar, please feel free to email me for further details.

A RESPONSIBLE BUYER/SELLER

It is vitally important for you, as a responsible buyer, to take all reasonable precautions prior to the investment of time/effort/capital, and prior to entering into a contract of sale. The following is a short explanation of *caveat emptor* and misrepresentation.

The above terms are normally applied to auction property from the outset. This I believe is changing with the advent of the diversity of purchasers interacting and indeed purchasing through the auction method.

I would say that up to approximately fifteen to twenty years ago, the auction industry was clad in a little mystery and misinformation, making it only accessible to a certain few — those with the knowledge and access to funds, or the bold and the brave. In recent years, the attraction of the auction, along with advances in technology and information sources, have allowed a far greater number and diversity of both buyer and seller to access the auction market.

The auction industry is changing slowly to meet the requirements of this new breed of seller and buyer but change to an area of the property industry which had pre-dated the estate agency is going to take some time. That said, I believe that the auction is the future.

CAVEAT EMPTOR

This is a Latin phrase and legal principle which loosely translates as 'let the buyer beware'. It is important to note that this principle is not restricted only to auction property sales — it applies in every property transaction and, more widely, forms part of almost every transaction you can think of, with the exception of services. The transaction for the most part must include the purchase of a 'thing' or the transfer of ownership of a 'thing'.

This is a legal principle that dates back centuries in English law and is still relied on today in the conveyancing process. It places the burden on the buyer to find out if there are any physical issues in the property or legal problems affecting the property.

Caveat emptor ends not when the seller makes an omission (remains silent), but when they attempt to, or succeed in covering up any physical or legally material issue affecting the property. If they do this, they run the risk of being sued, potentially for a fraudulent misrepresentation. In reality, the seller only has to disclose 'latent defects', a short list of which are below.

1 Any rights of way
2 Drainage
3 Underground pipeage
4 Restrictive covenants
5 Tenancy information
6 Land charges

MISREPRESENTATION

A misrepresentation is when a seller/their solicitor/their agent seeks to misinform a third party or induce that third party into purchasing a property either with inaccurate information, or by withholding vital information that the buyer could not reasonably be able to find for themselves.

There can be a very fine line between the principle of *caveat emptor* and misrepresentation. It is something that can appear blurry on the face of it, which is why property transactions involve such detailed due diligence processes including search packs, surveyor reports and PIFs (property information forms) or LIF (leasehold information forms), completed by the seller or their solicitor by proxy.

In conclusion, what does all this mean to you as a seller and as a buyer? It means that a robust due diligence process and an attentive and experienced solicitor will go a long way to ensuring that if there is an issue with a property, you are aware of that issue, you adjust your bidding accordingly and you have the capacity to work through whatever the issue may be, and create a position of profitability from it.

THE END

We hope you found reading this book educational, worthwhile and rewarding. Visit www.beforethehammerfalls.co.uk for more content

ACKNOWLEDGEMENTS

We would like to finish by thanking the most important people in our lives for supporting us whilst putting this book together. We cannot finish without a thank-you to our team, our publisher, partners of this book, RFB Solicitors, Mortgage Desk and Insurance Desk, and the network of support, all of whom have added to the success of this project in one way or another. A special thank-you to our reviewers, who not only took the time to read our book and review, but to offer advice and support.

@the.auction.pro I would like to acknowledge the following people in my life who have hugely contributed to the creation of this book and enabled me to focus on producing its content:

My parents: Dad, for instilling the passion for reading and learning in me; seeing him bring home a large bag of books from our local library every week (and reading all of it!). My Mum, for always ensuring we got what we needed to learn and prosper in life. My sisters, Ania, Gosia and Ewa, for being ready to support me in the business and in life whenever I asked them to, and for being close allies in growing up together.

My joint ventures partners, investors and clients who trusted me with the handling of their assets. Something which enabled me to be engaged in complex property transactions and to share all the learnings from that in this book.

Suresh Vagjianii, my first property mentor and boss, whom I met in the most unusual of circumstances... on a 10-day silent meditation retreat! Suresh spotted the potential in me to work alongside him in property and offered me a job when I came to London after my university. The learnings from that go well beyond property.

Jamie Royston and Andrew Binstock, directors of Auction House London, for the business partnership that has seen me buying or selling large volume of properties since the inception of AHL. And also, for being supportive of the book and allowing us to use the AHL premises over the weekends while we were writing the book.

Simon Zutshi, for creating an educational platform that allowed me to expand my confidence to do my own deals and partner up with other committed people!

Kamil Frost, a friend and business partner for his big thinking and for keeping me growing.

Tomasz Waszkiewicz, for being a person who makes a difference, someone who inspires me with his bold ideas and someone who always finds a way to have fun doing this.

Mahfuz Rahman, a solicitor and a close friend, who keeps inspiring me with his approach to law, business and life, and who at such a young age has become an incredibly accomplished solicitor.

Stephen Koehne, a very experienced property solicitor and a good friend, whose calm and measured approach combined with vast experience, has kept me grounded through a lot of challenging property transactions.

Jennifer Lin, an adventurous and driven property investor who has become a close partner and friend in my property journey.

Also all the people who I might have not listed here but who were a great contribution in my business and life. You know who you are, and I value and honour your presence in my life.

And finally, last but not least, Jay Howard, the co-writer of this book, a genius and someone who became a close friend, for being there on most of the weekends in the months of this book being written, sitting opposite me, and inspiring the content of the book being typed into a document! So many times in life, I might have ideas which takes time to become a reality but, being fortunate to have people like Jay around me, writing this book was so much easier!

@the.auction.insider I would like to finish by thanking the most important people in my life; firstly my wife Claudia for her endless love and unflinching belief in me; my mother who is no longer with us, but continues to be a massive inspiration to me and a drive for me to succeed; my original property mentor – although we are no longer in contact – thank you for making life a challenge; and for everyone whose name I haven't mentioned (I could probably write a whole new book, with just people's names) for supporting me whilst putting this book together.

I would also like to thank Jamie Royston and Andrew Binstock of Auction House London for their moral support in this endeavour.

I cannot finish without a thank-you to our team and network of support: Brendan Quinn, Mike Frisby, Ranjan Bhattacharya, Kam Dovedi, Diksesh Patel, Manni Chopra, Richard Woodstock, Mahfuz Rahman and Bindar Dosanjh, all of whom have added to the success of this project in one way or another. A special thank-you to our reviewers: David Sandeman, Angela Bryant and Richard Bowser, who not only took the time to read our book and review, but to offer additional advice and support.

I would like to thank our readers for making it to the end of this book. I hope that you have enjoyed the contents and, further, that this book will have enriched you in your ongoing property journey. If you have enjoyed the reading experience, I would like to ask you to recommend it to friends, family and colleagues as well as leaving a review on Amazon to ensure that as many people as possible see the book and benefit from its message.

A big thank-you to the market influencers and disruptors we call clients and investors: Ross Harper, Martin Skinner, Paul Higgs, Evan Maindonald, Adam Lawrence, Mark King, Samuel Leeds and Samuel Ikhinmwin, who are always a rich source of knowledge and experience and who continue to drive my passion in property ever forward.

Finally, and without a doubt a massive thank-you to my co-author, good friend and client Piotr Rusinek, who had the idea of writing this book and who invited me to be part of this project. This process has definitely brought us closer and has positively impacted our working relationship. It has increased the success of the properties being offered and sold and likewise, being purchased. Long may this relationship continue to flourish and grow.

Looking forward to the next book already...